CHANGE AND CONTINUITY

The Story of Sacred Heart Parish, Exeter

This book is dedicated to all the parishioners of

THE MINT CHAPEL

and

SACRED HEART CHURCH

Exeter

Published by Diocesan Trading Limited, © 2005
Registered in England: 2564900
VAT Reg. No. 585467003
Printed by Short Run Press Limited, Exeter, Devon
ISBN: 0-9551017-0-0

CHANGE & CONTINUITY

The Story of Sacred Heart Parish, Exeter

CONTENTS

Foreword by Monsignor Harry Doyle

FOREWORD

Monsignor Harry Doyle

"A bishop is not a bishop by himself but only in Catholic communion with those who were bishops before him, are bishops with him and will be bishops after him". Thus wrote the then Cardinal Ratzinger, now Pope Benedict XVI, in 1987.

If this is true of a bishop, how much more it is true of a parish priest, or indeed, a parish. A parish can only exist if it is in communion with the Diocese, with the other parishes of the Diocese and the wider church. The parish must also have a link with its past and give thanks to God for our predecessors who by their prayer and dedication did so much to build up the wonderful community that we have at present. We in our time have a duty to build on these foundations in order that future generations may be able to be sustained in their faith by the example that we have left them.

I am indebted to Professor Robert Leaper for agreeing to take on the task of compiling a faith history of the Sacred Heart parish. I thank him for the research he has undertaken and the tenacity with which he carried it out. In this age when the good done by former generations is often belittled, we should salute the fine men and women who did so much in the past for our community. The danger is that we forget even more than our great people. There are so many cultural, traditional values and qualities which are rapidly disappearing from memory. This book gives us a flavour of life in the past not just in the parish of the Sacred Heart but also in the city of Exeter, the Diocese of Plymouth and the Universal Church.

The title of the book, 'Change and Continuity', has a message in itself that while we give thanks for the past we live in the present. Just as our forebears while holding fast to the message of Christ changed and adapted to the times that they lived in, we too have to change and adapt to the Church and society of today. I hope that Professor Leaper's work will help us to understand more about the parish and the rich deposit of faith that has been passed down to us.

I warmly welcome this publication and recommend it to you.

AUTHOR'S PREFACE

In this short book we are concerned with the history, evolution and present dynamic of a Catholic parish. Inevitably we are obliged to consider briefly the environment in which it grew and in which it is now set. I have been able to draw upon some original sources, some secondary writings, on personal evidence from present parishioners and from witnesses in other Exeter churches. I list below the names of the many people for whose help I am indebted. The written sources are separately listed. Some of the material in this book was used in the booklet of the same title written in 1984. There have been so many amendments and additions that this is effectively a new publication.

This is a story about people in a place for a purpose. We start with a definition of two basic terms: *parish* and *community*.

In the current "Catechism of the Catholic Church" [36.1] (1994, Paragraph 2179) we read "A parish is a definite (sic) community of the Christian faithful established on a stable basis within a particular church; the pastoral care of the parish is entrusted to a pastor as its own shepherd under the authority of the diocesan bishop" (Codex Iuris Canonici 1983).

"It is the place where all the faithful can be gathered for the Sunday celebration of the Eucharist. The parish initiates the Christian people into the ordinary expression of the liturgical life; it gathers them together in this celebration; it teaches Christ's saving doctrine; it practises the charity of the Lord in good works and brotherly love."

In dealing with the network of relationships between parishioners, clergy, and the society around us we frequently encounter the word "community." It covers a wide range of contacts and is in danger of being so loosely used that it can become little more than a comforting epithet. We may too readily assume that membership of the Christian *communion* is of the same quality as belonging to communities of locality or of common interest. [41.1]

In examining our urban centre parish of the Sacred Heart it seems wise to be clear about the extent and nature of "community." The parish covers part of the urban centre, somewhat arbitrarily divided with Blessed Sacrament, Heavitree parish, but its catchment area extends to Rewe to the north, Tedburn St. Mary to the west, and Exminster and Kennford to the south-west. It has a boundary with Topsham parish, most of which is still within Exeter City limits. Clearly Sacred Heart Parish covers many quite distinct neighbourhoods. (A map of the boundaries of the three Catholic parishes within the area of Exeter City Council is in an appendix to this book).

> "*Community* is most usefully and
> precisely employed to refer to a
> limited area of living defined as
> such by the people in it, with
> reference to: common residence,
> common interest, and mutual
> inter-action and obligation." [41.1]

Is a parish a rather special kind of a "community?" To what extent does parish history influence "mutual inter-action and obligation?" Is awareness of change in society more important than a sense of continuity? These are some of the questions to whose discussion a modest parish book may contribute.

Increased occupational and geographic mobility (especially more car use) obliges us to modify the notion of a static parish peopled by a stable population - a concept which was more valid when Sacred Heart Church first opened in 1884, or when St. Thomas Church on Dunsford Road was built in 1938. We have to take account of social and economic changes when we worship and work together, and of the extent to which locality determines our social activity and our sense of belonging.[19]

"If members of the parish only meet at Sunday Mass it can be difficult to establish a real sense of parish community."[48] From experience in Sacred Heart parish one might comment that attendance at Mass and the importance given to welcoming newcomers provides the opportunity to join in common interest groups from which personal friendships or continued association often grow. (The analysis of role and function in different social networks is of course a commonplace of sociology and the subject of an enormous literature).[20, 46, 75]

Questions about effective relationships between local parish units and the rest of the Catholic Church pre-occupied participants at the National Pastoral Congress in Liverpool in 1980.[41.2] Seventeen years later a Diocesan Assembly in Plymouth Diocese involved delegates from almost all parishes, including Sacred Heart, Exeter. This Assembly led to a "Vision Statement" by the Bishop with a reformulation of obligations and engagement and to the setting up of a Diocesan Pastoral Council.[12] A welcome initiative in 2004 has been the promulgation of proposals for new Parish Pastoral Councils and for clearer lines of communication and answerability between them and church structures at deanery and diocesan levels. Significantly *The Tablet* embarked in May 2004 on a series of articles on "Parish Practice" edited by Carolyn Butler with the intention of chronicling new parish developments.

The Diocese is seen as the essential unit of the Church and strictly speaking the parish is a local branch of that diocese. The governance of the Diocese is according to Canon Law on a clearly Episcopal model rather than on one built up from the local parish.[4] Under Civil Law, however, the diocese is defined as a registered Charity governed by a board of trustees who "are appointed by the existing trustees but only with the Bishop's prior approval."[15.1]

It is predominantly from parishioners' contributions, from legacies or investment income that Diocesan resources (managed by the "curia") are derived. The annual report and accounts of the Diocese, which as a registered charity it is obliged to publish,[55] sets out the financial and human resources at the Diocese's disposal.

The basic principle of Catholic parish finance is that it should be self-supporting, covering its running costs, its repairs and maintenance and its clergy support. It finds the means to do this from collections, fund-raising, donations and legacies. As its contribution to diocesan finance each parish pays a levy based on dual precept factors - namely Mass attendance and a percentage of total parish income. In return staff are engaged at diocesan level to assist parishes in their essential work - in education, finance, formation and so on.[4]

Diocesan finance can also help parishes in the case of emergencies or urgent repairs beyond parish finances. Diocesan loans, as approved by the trustees, can be made available at 1% below base interest rate. Nationally the Guild of Ransom gives grants, through the Bishop, to needy parishes, the Guild's income being in turn derived from membership fees, including some from Exeter parishioners.[P.22, 10]

There are, of course, other calls upon parishioners' generosity – for example, for education, child care and child protection, CAFOD, Social and Recreational activities. Some are part of the formal Diocesan structures; some have their own independent governance and work harmoniously with the diocesan curia. In other bodies, Catholic parishioners are prominent in their work but they are ecumenical Christian bodies, or organisations not specifically Christian but carrying out practical work with which any Christian would be fully justified in engaging.[56] These may be thought of as two models of Catholic parish action - the ghetto model and the Catholic citizenship model.[14, 38, 51, 80] We further explore this debate in later chapters.

Mainly for the purposes of clergy conferences - but to a limited extent for inter-parish action of various kinds - the diocese is divided into five deaneries. Exeter Deanery is one of these into which Devon is divided, being a somewhat arbitrary slice of territory from Exmouth eastwards to the Dorset border, from the Exe estuary to Plymouth Deanery, and north to Hartland, Ilfracombe and the Somerset border.[P.10] A survey of parish opinion taken at Sunday masses by the Parish Pastoral Council in 2003 showed that of greatest significance to most parishioners was the parish, the Diocese next, and the Deanery of hardly any significance at all. We return to the work of the Parish Pastoral Council in Chapter 10.

A brief reference to recent discussion of the role and significance of the parish unit in the Church of England seems helpful. As the Anglican Church is a national church, so the parish unit is inherent in the economic and administrative structure of the nation.[4] At the Reformation parishes were asked to provide for the poor and to undertake a host of local administrative duties. Reform in the nineteenth century established parish councils as part of local government, distinguishing town from rural life.[4, 70] In the Anglican Diocese of Exeter the Wilds report, *Moving on in Mission and Ministry* (2004) sets out proposals for "sustainable mission communities" with regular lay participation and specified amounts of licensed ministry. This must involve more sharing and more devolution of responsibility.

Simon Jenkins in his compilation of "England's Thousand Best Churches" on the other hand, pleads for the continued recognition of the parish church as the repository of a way of life ever to be retained and valued. Nicholas Orme further clarifies the role of *minsters*, particularly with reference to their origins between 500 and 1050 AD, concluding "The word 'minster' is therefore useful today, because it indicates a large church served by several clergy without implying what sort of life they were following."[51.2, 54, 70, 74]

Platt in his study of the Parish Churches of Medieval England has a whole chapter on "The Community of the Parish"; he comments that church furnishings and monuments are a clear reflection of the social and economic structure of the society of which they are a part. Spencer concludes "It is time to re-think the English parish and to consider seriously how its future might lie in the long-dormant Anglo-Saxon minster system."[70]

I acknowledge gratefully help with proof reading given by Valerie Espig and Sheila Lasok, and related help by Eric Berggren. I am also indebted to those listed below. The responsiblity for the final text - including errors and omissions - is the author's.

Acknowledgements are readily made in particular to the following: Reverend Canon F. Balment, Jean Bendall, Robert Bendall, Shirley Blaskett, Mary Bownes, Reverend Canon N. Collings, Reverend Father Keith Collins, Reverend Canon Paul Cummins, John Curran, Nick Day, Reverend Monsignor Harry Doyle, Raymond Fennessy, Dr. Tegwyn Harris, Harold Holding, Professor Christopher Holdsworth, Reverend Canon Bernard Jaffa, Dennis Lambert, Elizabeth Leaper, Susan Leaper, Laurence McWilliam, Sister Edward Mary Milsom, Sister Guy-Marie Montagne, Cecilia O'Keeffe, Fred O'Keeffe, Professor Nicholas Orme, Kathleen O'Shaughenessy, Peggy O'Sullivan, Martin Overy, Nigel Power, Maureen Sleeman, Reverend Canon Christopher Smith, Hilda Swinburne, Lorna Till, Canon M. Walsh, Reverend John Webb, John Woolcott. Of all these I must single out the late Laurence McWilliam ("Mr. Mac") for his extensive manuscript notes about Sacred Heart Parish. Monsignor Harry Doyle has encouraged open research into the parish archives and sustained my application to writing up a selection of their contents. The diocesan archivist, Canon Christopher Smith, has generously allowed consultation. Canon Paul Cummins made available precious records of Dr. George Oliver in the library of the University Catholic Chaplaincy. The sisters of Mount St. Mary's Convent made me welcome in their library and let me consult their convent Annals. I have been able to research in the Library of the Devon and Exeter Institution and in Exeter Cathedral Library.

For her patience and efficiency in dealing with the present text and seeing it through to publication I am greatly indebted to Susan Berggren.

Robert Leaper, 2005

CHAPTER 1

A Guide to the Fabric of the Church

The church celebrated its centenary in 1984. The corner stone was laid by Bishop Vaughan of Plymouth in 1883. The church is built on the site of the former Bear Inn, which belonged to the Abbots of Tavistock since 1481. The first post-Reformation record of a Catholic Church in Exeter is of a chapel in the Mint, near the remains of St. Nicholas Priory. The chapel was recorded as a place of worship in 1791, and it was replaced by the present church when money was raised by a committee of local Catholics under the chairmanship of their Diocesan Bishop. The architect was Leonard Stokes in partnership with C. E. Ware.

Fig 1 *High Altar, sanctuary, reredos and rood screen*

From the bottom of the church, you look up to the neo-Gothic nave with its oak vault. The roof above it had to be replaced in 1989 - at considerable cost. The left aisle is wider than the right, the transept is truncated, and the sanctuary large with a fine stone reredos and two side chapels. The church's dimensions are: outside length 145 ft; width 90 ft; height from floor to roof 60 ft. The inside walls are of varied stone from Poccombe quarries with Bath stone dressing. The columns up the aisles are of

Portland stone with brown Poccombe stone above. The large wrought-iron rood screen with its crucifixion scene above it was given by Miss Middleton of London in 1886. The invocation spelt out in wrought iron above the screen reads: "Per mortem tuam libera nos Domine" (By thy death set us free, O Lord). The four statues high up at the ends of the rood screen are of: St. Sidwell, St. George, Edward the Confessor and a figure about whose identity there has been some speculation. Examination of the parish archives has been enhanced by close-up photography by Dr. Tegwyn Harris and by expert guidance from Mr. Keith Barker of Exeter Cathedral. St. Juthwara, St. Walburga, St. Bridget, St. Brigid, and Queen Edith (spouse of Edward the Confessor) have all been suggested as candidates for recognition. The final consensus is that the statue is indeed that of St. Walburga (as proposed by Canon Hobson) and that she holds a container of holy oil, has a crozier of some sort by her side, a crown at her feet and (obviously) a halo behind a head covered in a veil.

Fig 2 *St. Edward the Confessor, St. Walburga*
[Tegwyn Harris]

As you stand with your back to the main west door, the bell-tower is on your left. It houses one bell, hung in 1884 and dedicated to St. Boniface. From the outside you will notice that the tower is somewhat squat; it was originally intended to add a spire. Thanks to prompt and courageous action by clergy and fire-watchers the church escaped almost unscathed the fire-bomb attack during the war in 1942 which destroyed the city centre.

Two twin West windows light the church as does the large clerestory above the nave. Internal buttresses of an unusual design support the thrust of the roof. The whole church seems a good example of Victorian Neo-Gothic. It has some oddities in construction but also a comfortable consistency. It has seating for 400 people.

On the right of the main West door is a pietà statue. This was given in 1926 by Harry Bayley (goalie for Exeter City Football Club) as a thanksgiving for his Silver Wedding. Beyond it is the corner baptistery. There are good wrought-iron gates and rails with the inscription "Janua Caeli" (gate of heaven). A brass plaque on the wall records the gift of the baptistery rails in memory of a former M.P. of Exeter until 1874. The font itself is modern, and a stained glass window above it is in memory of the church architect and his wife.

Fig 3 *The Baptistery*   [Tegwyn Harris]

Up the south aisle past the confessionals on the right is the stone pulpit with miniature panels and appropriate exhortations. At the top of the aisle is the St. Joseph altar, the gift of Mrs Alexandra Knight of Axminster in 1881. Note the inlaid wooden floor blocks with a similar pattern to those on the main sanctuary. They are of Italian origin of unusually intricate design; they were repaired and replaced under a Manpower Services Commission scheme in 1985.

The front altar rails have enamel painted depictions of Christ's suffering and death and an inscription describing the holy Eucharist. The mass altar is in the centre of the sanctuary. The old high altar behind it dates from 1906 and is confected in marble and alabaster. The ornate stone reredos depicts on the left, St. John Fisher (with axe and block); St. Peter (with keys), on the right; St. John the Evangelist (an eagle at his feet); St. Cuthbert Mayne (martyred at Launceston). The four carved panels show on the left, the miracle of loaves and fishes and the Holy Eucharist, and on the right the Sacred Heart and Manna from Heaven. The decoration immediately above the tabernacle is in alabaster by the Reverend Alexander Scoles from Bridgwater. The rear altar itself is of stone from Beer quarry and it is decorated in marble and alabaster. The stations of the cross around the walls are painted on zinc in Munich and were given to the church in 1886 by Miss Middleton. In the sanctuary there are two murals painted on canvas high up on each of the side walls. One depicts Christ the High Priest and the other James Tuberville, last Catholic Bishop of Exeter, who was deprived of his office in 1559. Above the altar rails are two recent statues - one of them of our Lady of Sorrows and the other of the Sacred Heart, a gift to the church from Canon Hobson on the occasion of the silver jubilee of his priesthood in 1885.

Continue across to the Lady Chapel where on the left wall in front is a plaque to "Edward Petre, aviator." He was the son of Mr. and Mrs. Petre of "Tor Bryan" Ingatestone, and a cousin of Lord Petre of Thorndon Hall. The Petre family had Devon connections. Edward Petre was killed at Marske-by-the-Sea, Yorkshire while flying a monoplane from Brooklands to Edinburgh. A subscription from parishioners and from the Petre family paid for new stalls, to the design of Mr. Edward Ware to be executed by Herbert E. Read of Sidwell St. and installed in the chancel in 1913. The stained glass windows above depict the definition of the doctrine of the Immaculate Conception. The altar is marble, with stone carvings showing the annunciation (centre) and the assumption and coronation of Mary on either side. The reredos shows the marriage feast at Cana and the crucifixion.

Fig 4 The Lady Altar

The St. Boniface altar is at the top of the North aisle and is immediately below the St. Boniface window, which depicts scenes from the life of the saint. The saints whose carved statues adorn the altar are all local or at least have connections with St. Boniface, though they are little known in the twenty-first century. [(P.4)]

They have been traced in the Oxford Dictionary of Saints by David Hugh Farmer (1987 edition), Oxford University Press. Due acknowledgements are made to this excellent source, which has a useful introduction to the cult of saints, and a very wide and scholarly coverage of English saints and of "the most important and representative saints of Ireland, Scotland and Wales." The list of saints whose statues are on the Boniface altar are given in the Annexe to this chapter, and details of them can be found in Farmer's book already referred to.

Fig 5 *Statue of St. Thomas More*

A new list of saints' feast days was published with the approval of the Vatican in June, 2000. [(31)] The new list re-asserted the importance of some traditional English saints who seemed to have fallen out of fashion recently - for example, St. George. The publication of "Saints of the English Calendar" under the editorship of Marcus Holden presents summaries of the lives of 45 saints and lists places to visit associated with them. The list includes St. Willibrord, St. Edward the Confessor, St. Thomas More, and St. John Fisher all of whom are referred to in connection with Sacred Heart Parish. The saints are also listed in celebration of the Church's year in a way which encourages specific reference to them on their Feast Days. "We are blessed with a great crowd of witnesses across more than 1500 years" comments Holden. [(31)] The Catechism refers to "the long history of the saints whom the liturgy celebrates in the rhythms of the sanctoral cycle." [(36.1)] We are reminded of the large number of saints sanctified by Pope John Paul II.

The organ loft in the South transept is used by the church choir on Sundays, Feast Days, weddings and funerals. The organ is a remarkable instrument. A summary of the full description provided by Dr. Tegwyn Harris, the current church organist, is as follows:

"The organ was built in 1893 by Hele and Company who had premises in Bartholomew Street (later Preston Street), at the time. The organ case was designed by Mr. Thompson, the manager of the company, who was a member of the Parish of the Sacred Heart.

There can be no doubt that the Sacred Heart organ is one of the finest in Exeter - it is also one of the most fascinating in terms of its mechanisms. The whole action of the organ is pneumatic - that is, wind-driven, so that every function which ultimately results in a sound is based upon the opening and closing of leather bellows ("motors" in organ-builder's language).

Perhaps one of the strangest aspects of the original design of the organ is that the smaller wind-carrying tubes (wind-trunks) consist of ½ inch lead gas piping. This fact caused a good deal of consternation when it came to light during the restoration of 1985 since such piping is no longer available. However, a quick-witted member of the rebuilding team spotted that the outside diameter of the lead piping is the same as the inside diameter of modern metal-reinforced plastic hose-piping which, of course, will never wear out. Thus, it will be seen that this magnificent musical instrument which started its life dependent upon domestic gas-piping, continues to make music with the aid of a hose-pipe!

The organ, as we now have it, was expertly restored by the then Taunton-based organ-builders - George Osmond and Co. However, by 1984, playing the organ for Sunday Mass had become something of a lottery since it was impossible to predict from one choir practice to the next service exactly which bits would still be working!

The original instrument was blessed by Bishop Vaughan on the Feast of the Sacred Heart, 1893 and the restored organ was blessed by the Rev. Fr. Keith Collins at sung Mass on Sunday, August 4th, 1985."

The choir loft was completely closed-in until the early nineteen seventies. The wooden fronting was then removed, so that the choir did not have to sing for services in such claustrophobic conditions. A small stone transomed window in the stairway up to the organ loft dates from 1495 and was retrieved from the rubble when the church was built on the site of the Bear Inn.

The stained glass windows down the side of the north aisle were installed to commemorate the golden jubilee of the church's opening. They show the Sacred Heart of Jesus, and the inspiration of St. Margaret Mary to stimulate devotion to it among Catholics. The last one shows St. Nicholas giving alms to needy people, and is a link between this church and the old Mint church near St. Nicholas Priory. It recalls the long witness of Dr. George Oliver who was in charge of the Mission Church in the Mint.

At the bottom of the church is a statue of Christ the King, brought from Dublin Eucharistic Congress in 1932 by Fr. T. Barney. It was carried through Exeter streets during parish processions. Immediately inside the tower door is a statue of St. Patrick. The large "mission" crucifixion on the bottom wall dates from about 1890. Next to it is a modest war memorial tablet, commemorating those who died in two world wars.

Next to the side door is the repository from which religious articles, candles or greetings cards may be purchased.

The narthex opens out from the West door as you leave. It is large but its potential use is reduced by the awkward slope of the land on which it is built. Of Sacred Heart Church, Nicholas Pevsner writes of its "rewarding interior with quite dramatic contrasting spaces, a low vaulted narthex and a broad and lofty nave."

There is slight inconsistency in the name given to the parish and to the church building in 'Change and Continuity.' Should it be "Sacred Heart Church" or "Church of the Sacred Heart" or some other variant of the basic dedication? The church is listed in the Diocesan Yearbook as "Sacred Heart." The inscription on vellum at the laying of the first stone refers to "this church dedicated to the Sacred Heart of Our Lord Jesus Christ," (see page 59). The current parish priest gives his definitions in his foreword. A random sampling of regular parishioners' customary definitions of the name of the church produced some variation in replies, the one most favoured being simply "Sacred Heart."

In this chapter we have dealt very briefly with the fabric of the church building. It is of course built as a fitting centre in which the worship of God may be offered; it is not a museum or an interesting historic artefact. In the next chapters we deal with its history, its current use and its future.

In the two years before he died in March 2002, John Curran set about the task of thoroughly cleaning the interior stonework of the church. He undertook the work almost single-handed, and succeeded in cleaning statues and altars as well as walls and pillars. The bright interior of the church is in no small measure due to John Curran's work.

References for this chapter will be found at:

P.1, P.10, P.12, P.19, P.22
and
21, 24, 29, 30.5, 31, 33.3, 34, 37, 67, 71

For the classic reference book, the reader is referred to:

A History of Architecture by Banister Fletcher, Batsford.
(noted with thanks to Dennis Lambeth, architect and parishioner)

ANNEXE

Saints Commemorated on the St. Boniface Altar

ST. BONIFACE

(Winfrith, c675 - 754)

St. Boniface was born in Crediton, baptised Winfrith, later named Boniface, educated at an Exeter monastery, then at Nursling (Hants.) ordained a priest when aged thirty. He was a successful preacher and teacher, and chosen as envoy from the Wessex synod to the Archbishop of Canterbury. He was chosen to go on missionary work to Frisia and was then elected Abbot of Nursling on return to England. However he preferred to return to Frisia to help Willibrord, then to Hesse and Bavaria. He was consecrated bishop in 722 and archbishop in 732. Helping reform the Church in France, he returned to Frisia in later life and was killed with his companions near Dokkum in 754, his body being taken to Fulda. He is the patron of the Diocese of Plymouth and is revered by the Church of England Diocese of Exeter. There is an ecumenical Boniface Centre in Crediton.

Front of Altar

Stand facing the altar. There are two large statues at the front - St. Sidwell (left) and St. Juthwara (right), and eight smaller statues. Start with the lower small statue on the left of St. Boniface, and follow the statues around in a clockwise direction.

ST. BURCHARD (d. 754)

ST. SIDWELL (Sithewelle, Sativola, dates uncertain)

ST. WALBURGA (Walpurgis, Vaubourg, d. 779)

ST. WINNIBALD (d. 761)

ST. GREGORY III (d. 741)

ST. LULLUS (c710 - 786)

ST. JUTHWARA (dates uncertain)

The large statue at the right front of the altar is of St. Juthwara.

ST. WILLIBALD (d. 786)

ST. RICHARD (d. 720)

St. Richard was father of Willibald, Winnibald and Walburga.

ST. WILLEHAD (d. 789)

Right Side of Altar

(Facing Our Lady Altar)

ST. GREGORY II (d. 731)

On the top of the right side of the altar is St. Gregory II.

ST. WILLIBRORD (638 - 739)

Below St. Gregory II is located St. Willibrord.

Left Side of Altar

(Facing down the Church)

ST. EOBAN (d. 754)

ST. LIOBA (d. 782)

In a leaflet at Sacred Heart Church St. Lioba was confused with St. Elide, a male hermit whose remains are said to be on St. Helen's Island on Scilly. (See Nicholas Orme, The Saints of Cornwall, Oxford University Press, 2000)

Above the altar is the large stained glass window to St. Boniface of Crediton, showing scenes from his life including his martyrdom in Germany.

CHAPTER 2

Foundations

About 49AD the second Augustan legion of Vespasian pushed the Roman occupation of Britain westward; moving on from Dorset, it conquered the small, but strategic, settlement by a river inhabited by the tribe of the Dumnonii and today known as Exeter. The Celtic name Eisca is said to refer to a river abounding in fish; hence Isca Dumnoniorum. [27.1]* Aileen Fox, the academic authority on Roman Exeter, interprets the tribal name as derived from the Celtic word dumno meaning its land or territory, and the Celtic word *Wysc* as referring to a river (found elsewhere in slightly different forms). Earlier variations of the city's name included Excester, as used by Camden in 1607. Fox divides the known history of Roman Exeter into three structural phases:

    (i) The military settlement   circa 45 - 75 AD
    (ii) The open city   circa 75 - 160
    (iii) The walled city   from the second century onwards [27.2]

It is important to bear in mind the topography of Exeter. [5, 33.3] Its main thoroughfare stands on a ridge. There is a comparatively plentiful supply of water from wells. [45] There is a fairly steep slope down to a natural landing-place on the navigable river. This means that South Street is a hill running down to the river - a fact which determines various features of Sacred Heart Church and its adjoining presbytery, as we shall comment on later. It also obliges the modern parishioners to puff up and down South Street to come to church on foot.

This is not the place for a potted history of Exeter. There are ample sources for that history in several published works, which are noted in the list of references. [7, 10, 30.5, 33.1 & .3, 42, 50.3, 62.2, 72, 76.1] This chapter contains a short selection of references to the environment of the Sacred Heart parish in Exeter's South Street. Previously known as Southgate Street, it was the most important entrance to the city. The large South Gate stood a few hundred yards below where the Sacred Heart Church is now situated.

The South Gate later incorporated the city prison - a building which has been described as "one of the foulest holes in England." [33.1] It was demolished in 1819, and is commemorated by a blue plaque on the pillar in lower South Street at the rear entrance to the Southgate Hotel.

To return to the Roman occupation: Hoskins [33.1] writes that the Dumnonii tribe made their peace with the Romans, who recognised Isca Dumnoniorum as the tribal

---

* Taylor, Isaac, Words and Places, J. M. Dent, 1936.

capital. The Romans built a bank around the town about 120 AD. This was superseded by a wall, the line of which was followed by the medieval city walls. Those walls run but a few hundred yards from Sacred Heart Church today. [72] Hoskins concedes that we know little about the Roman street plan but that there is clear evidence that the Forum (or market place) lay between South Street and Milk Street (today called Market Street at the junction of South Street and Fore Street). "This was the heart of Roman Exeter," wrote Hoskins, "and here lay most of the important public buildings." [33.1] Aileen Fox supplemented her studies of Roman Exeter [27.2] with a booklet written at the time of the 1971 excavations, following the demolition of St. Mary Major Church at the West Front of the Cathedral. Fox is rather more specific about the lay-out of the Roman city; "crossed by a Roman grid of well-metalled streets fronted by shops and houses built of stone or half-timbered." The Celtic inhabitants do not seem to have made it into a fortified settlement. After the campaign of 44 AD under Vespasian, the Romans built strategic forts, the remains of one of which were found in South Street in 1964. Exeter seems to have been still under Roman military control by the end of Emperor Nero's reign in 68 AD. By 75 - 80 the Roman troops were withdrawn for service in Wales and in Scotland. [10]

There followed the period of the "open city" during which the Dumnonii were a self-governing tribal group under the Imperial Roman rule. Fox also identifies a native settlement which had developed "in the area north of the fort and to the west of the present South Street." [27.2] The excavated remains of this settlement show evidence of early metal working and domestic goods trading as an adjunct to a military post; "a prosperous township in embryo developed in Exeter." [27.2]

The authors of a study of Exeter coinage [2] comment that considerable numbers of bronze coins of the Emperor Claudius have been found locally and that probably some of them had been struck in the Exeter area. Exeter City Museum has had displays of artefacts from the period of the Roman occupation and from that of the following Saxon Kingdom. Erskine writes: "By the last quarter of the fourth century Roman urban institutions had declined, and the fifth century can be regarded as a sub-Roman period, during which the Roman Forum came to be occupied by a cemetery, after the town had decayed and became largely depopulated, perhaps in the fifth, but possibly as late as the sixth century." [24] To several Exeter historians it seems likely that some remains of a Roman basilica were used to build a Christian chapel. [33.3, 24] It is not clear at what point Christianity came here, but it is known that one of the earliest signs left to us was found in South Street in 1946 when the shard of a cooking pot was discovered bearing the Christian symbol - "Chi Rho," the first two Greek letters of the name of Christ. "The pot was probably used to take offerings of food and drink to a church or Christian meeting place" [27.1] and it is estimated to date from the first half of the fourth century A.D. It would not be too fanciful to regard it as symbolic of Christian continuity in South Street, Exeter.

Close by the Forum were the Thermae (Baths), some remains of which were discovered in the Deanery garden in 1934, while in 1953 conduits from it were found in Bear Street, the narrow street running up the side of Sacred Heart Church, leading to the Deanery and Cathedral. The widening of South Street in 1951 led to the discovery of more extensive remains of a classic example of Roman baths. [27.2] (South Street overlaid the site of some Roman buildings). Further discoveries were made during the excavations at the West Front of the Cathedral in 1971. [10]

We may justly conclude that the plot of ground on which Sacred Heart Church and presbytery have been built has been in the very thick of things ever since the Roman occupation. The Romano-British civilization began to go downhill after a series of Barbarian attacks in 367 AD and the Forum was abandoned by about 390 AD. As we shall see, the erection of a post-Reformation church on this ground had to wait until the nineteenth century. Its predecessor chapel was founded further up South Street in the area known as the Mint in the grounds of St. Nicholas Priory. Before we reach that part of the parish story we must traverse the Saxon period and the centuries of civic administration, much influenced by religious differences and reconciliations.

CHAPTER 3

Christians in Exeter until 1536

Hoskins and Orme both document the Roman withdrawal in the early fifth century AD. Somewhat dramatically, Hoskins writes that after that date: "There is a total silence in the history of Exeter for almost three hundred years: not a single reference in any document anywhere, not a coin or a piece of pottery, not a fragment of a building." [33.1]

We can see clearly the centrality of the Christian faith when the Roman Empire grew weak and crumbled as it was to the Church that Christians grew accustomed to turn for support - and even for survival. The fate of Christians in Exeter - as elsewhere in Britain - had of course during the Roman occupation depended on policies followed throughout the Roman Empire. This meant persecution, followed by toleration in 313 under the Emperor Constantine. As Orme notes, we do not know for certain what happened in Exeter at that date [51.1] but it is quite possible that the town "acquired a congregation, a church and even a bishop." A cemetery dating probably from the middle of the fifth century was excavated close to the site of the present Cathedral during the nineteen seventies as already recorded, [10] and the graves in it appear to be of Christians. Many Celtic saints came to the South-West peninsula from Wales and Ireland during the sixth century, but details of their missionary work and of the co-operation with Christians of an earlier foundation remain very sketchy. [51.1] Their presence certainly left its mark on Cornwall - in place names, church dedications and linguistic culture. In Devon the Celtic influence was less emphatic (but note St. Petrock's Church, a close neighbour to present day Sacred Heart); and it was soon overlaid by Saxon influence reflected in the commemoration of Saints familiar to their culture.

The introduction to Ingram's presentation of the Anglo-Saxon Chronicle [33] refers to "two substantial monuments to England's early history" - Domesday Book and the Saxon Chronicle. The Chronicle makes clear that the Saxons arrived in this country in the mid fifth century and the Chronicle traces their story till 1154. There were certainly Christian Saxons in Exeter in about 690 because Winfrith (later Boniface) entered an Abbey here which had a Saxon Abbot at its head. His remarkable life - and that of his contemporaries - is recounted in a variety of sources. [31, 67, 71] Although the Saxons were nominally Christians by the end of the seventh century, there seems to have been some conflict between them and the Britons who maintained many of the Celtic Christian traditions. [51.2]

The Chronicle contains some references to Exeter. In 877 AD, "This year came the Danish army into Exeter from Wareham; whilst the navy sailed West about, they met with a great mist at sea, and there perished one hundred and twenty ships at

Swanage. Meanwhile King Alfred, with his army, rode after the cavalry as far as Exeter; but he "could not overtake them before their arrival in the fortress, where they could not be come at." [3] Another Danish raid in Exeter is recorded in 894. Later in 1003 yet another Danish attack is said to have "demolished" Exeter. The city was caught up in conflict between Norse invaders and local citizens, who are later recorded in 1067 as having surrendered the city to King William I "because the thanes had betrayed them." [3]

It may well have been the danger of attack from raiders that was part of the reason for the earnest request by Bishop Leofric to transfer the seat of the Bishop from Crediton to the more securely fortified city of Exeter. [7] At any rate Pope Leo IX agreed to the transfer. Leofric was duly installed in 1050 (probably on St. Peter's Day) in a sparsely furnished Cathedral but with great ceremony. The Bishop was led into the Cathedral on his right by King Edward and on his left by Queen Edith to his episcopal throne "in the presence of my great men and kinsfolk, my nobles and chaplains." [7] George Oliver was much later to describe the scene as "as an immense concourse of the nobility and dignified clergy." [50.2] Appropriately there is a statue at the end of the metal rood screen in Sacred Heart Church representing King Edward. Holdsworth comments that the formal approval of the move from Crediton to Exeter indicated the growth of power of the papacy "whose interests were not always the same as those of the monarchy, although Exeter was not a place where their interests were so opposed that violent clashes occurred, as at Canterbury." [51.2]

King Athelston came to Exeter in about 932 and ordered that a monastery be built in honour of St. Mary and St. Peter and that it be instituted as a secular minster. [24] In 968 King Edgar appears to have established a colony of monks in the place of the secular minster. [51.2]

"The chief centres of religion in the British Isles in the period 500 to 1050 were churches served by groups of clergy living communally," writes Orme. Such churches were called "minsters" by the Anglo-Saxons and might be of different types, ranging from monasteries following a formal monastic rule to groups of clergy living a more worldly existence. Those who lived in the second type were generally referred to as clerks or priests. Domesday Book (1086) listed fourteen probable minsters in Devon, four of which were founded or endowed by Kings, including that in Exeter. A parish consisted of the territories accredited to each minster; a system well established by the tenth century. There were several parish churches in medieval Exeter but the Cathedral had the monopoly of funerals and had also a number of local guilds affiliated to it. [51.2] Nevertheless Leofric found the Cathedral in 1050 poorly endowed, and he spent considerable effort and personal gifts on the Cathedral. He also established a group of canons who were to live communally and serve the reformed institution. [24]

There is not a space in this short book on the history and background of Sacred Heart Church to attempt a description of what has been called "The Decorated Cathedral par excellence (which) displays greater stylistic continuity than any other pre-Reformation English Cathedral except Salisbury. To step into Exeter Cathedral is to enjoy another of the supreme architectural pleasures of England." [16] There are full and scholarly accounts of the history and development of Exeter Cathedral, particularly by Erskine and her colleagues and there are good visitor guides - both in human and in printed form! - in the Cathedral itself. [24, 37, 51.1, 77] Sacred Heart Church was built under the shadow of the Cathedral and the congregations of the two, despite bitter differences in the past, today share in many common inter-Christian activities. The Deanery is but a stone's throw across narrow Bear Street from the Catholic Church and Presbytery; the residents of each domain live in harmony.

We have mentioned the rood screen statue in Sacred Heart Church commemorating King Edward's and Queen Edith's part in installing Bishop Leofric in 1080. Leofric died in 1072 and was buried in his church, being succeeded by the first Norman bishop.

We now turn to another embellishment of the Sacred Heart Church in stained glass and in statuary which commemorates the life and martyrdom of a remarkable man - Saint Boniface (born Winfrith) whose pre-occupation and dedication was the evangelisation of territories in both Germany and the Netherlands. [21, 67] His life's work was marked by missionary activity. [P.4] For him and his associates England was not considered a beneficiary of missions from outside its boundaries, but rather a source of evangelistion to other countries within Europe.* In 719 Pope Gregory II gave him the name Bonifatius in place of his baptismal name Winfrith. [21, 51.2, 67]

The stained glass windows in the north transept of Sacred Heart church tell the Boniface story in pictorial form. The windows illustrate six episodes in the life of St. Boniface: permission from his sick father to enter monastic life in Exeter; an apparition of an angel to Winfrith, as he was originally named, promising a harvest of souls and a martyr's crown; his visit to Rome for the Pope's blessing; his consecration as a bishop by Pope Gregory II; his reverence to St. Peter's tomb; and his felling of the Great Thor's oak tree sacred to the heathens of Frisia. The central window shows Boniface in full pontifical vestments and the window at the base shows his martyrdom. He was killed near Dokkum in the Frisian district of the North Netherlands where "the unconverted of the region, and renegades among the baptised, conceivably instigated by those hostile to Boniface in Cologne or further afield were physically attacking this exposed contingent of the spiritual army of Christ …. Boniface, protected till the last by others, finally fell, his skull shattered by a Frisian sword." [67] The bodies were recovered, the killers were pursued and killed, and after considerable discussion about the place of rest for his body, Boniface was buried at Fulda (in Hessen) where his shrine is revered today. The story of his early missions to Frisia, his frequent and lengthy journeys throughout what is modern Western Germany, Netherlands and Luxembourg, his visits to Rome and his interventions in political disputations which affected his missionary work - all this

---

* See especially Plymouth Diocesan Yearbook, 2005.

shows the boy born Winfrith in Crediton and educated in Exeter to have been a model for the evangelisation obligation laid on all Christians. "St. Boniface, glory of Devon, Apostle of Germany, martyr" is the patron of the Catholic Diocese of Plymouth and is revered by the Anglican Diocese of Exeter. [51.2, 67]

Fig 6 *St. Boniface Altar and Window*

Boniface was also remarkable for his ability to draw others into the missionary work in Germany. Many of the Saxon saints associated with the works, or known as local saints, are commemorated in the Altar below the Boniface window already described. (A full description of the statues adorning the Boniface altar and its reredos is given in the annexe to Chapter 1.) Suffice it to record here that there are small statues on the altar in addition to St. Boniface, of eleven saints associated with his work in Frisia and Germany. There are also two well-known local saints, St. Sidwell and her sister St. Juthwara, both of whom are said in local legend to have been killed at the instigation of wicked step-mothers.

The links between Exeter and the small town of Crediton have already been mentioned. They have persisted to the present day. There is now an ecumenical St. Boniface Centre in Crediton and in 2004 the anniversary of Boniface's martyrdom in 754 was celebrated in a series of events there, including a Catholic diocesan pilgrimage. There are regular pilgrimages from Germany and the Netherlands. Catholic links between the two population centres were renewed when priests from Exeter went to Crediton to say mass for a growing Catholic population; this led to the building of a permanent church in 1924. The chaplain to Exeter University has now for many years also served as parish priest to Crediton. [21]

There have been bishops of Crediton from 909 down to 1050 when Leofric transferred to Exeter. There is today a Suffragan Bishop of Crediton with membership of the Cathedral College of Canons.

"Between 1050 and 1307 things were to change very considerably, so that by the end something very much like the present organisation existed." [51.2] Holdsworth attributes this to various factors: population growth, wider trading exchanges, early industries as, for example in Exeter serge manufacture, the imposition of a firm Norman rule - especially after the siege of Exeter by William in 1068. [33.1] Exe Island had become by the end of the twelfth century a hive of industry and the city a thriving commercial centre below the Norman Castle on the hill of Rougemont, with an emerging system of local administration, including a mayor from 1205.

From all these changes some pattern of ecclesiastical continuity emerged first in 1222 when parish boundaries were drawn within the already established diocese. Intermediary structures - archdeaconries and rural deaneries - and specific Cathedral offices came to be established as adaptations in Church life to the changes in social and political structures. [39, 54, 65]

There were many monastic establishments in Exeter, several within the present boundaries of Sacred Heart parish (see map). The Dominicans or Blackfriars, (Ordo Praedicatorum) came to Exeter in about 1232 during the episcopate of William Brewer (after whom a door in the Cathedral south aisle is named). The Friars built a house and church with stone from a quarry near the castle and the church was consecrated by Bishop Bronscombe in November 1259. [33.3, 50.1, 69] It stood in what is now Catherine Street, with its own gate into the Cathedral Close. The Dominicans seem to have been involved in many complicated negotiations with both the mayor and the Dean and Chapter of the Cathedral. These included the classic case in 1301 of the quarrel over who should receive and bury the body of Henry Raleighe, Knight. Hooker comments that "the said corpse lay so long unburyed that it stanke and the

Canons were driven to bury the same in St. Peter's Churche." The quarrel dragged on until 1306 when the tiny parish church of St. Pancras was involved as was the widow of Henry Raleighe, one Johanna, whose wishes seem to have been respected rather late in the affair. After appeals heard in Oxford University, Pope Boniface VIII issued in 1303 a mandate to the Bishop of Bath and Wells to protect the rectors and curates of parishes in the city and diocese of Exeter against attempts of the Friars Preachers and Minors to infringe them by preaching, hearing confessions and burying the dead without their leave. The Blackfriars were responsible for a small school of theology and many well-known scholars were connected with it. Cardinal Gasquet estimated the average number of Friars per friary as nine [69] but at the date of suppression (1538) Exeter Dominican Friary was said to have 14 friars. [69] In the following year Lord John Russell obtained a royal gift of the whole house and church; he changed the priory into Bedford House, a mansion described approvingly by Leland. [50.2] The site was built on later as Bedford Circus and 1831 the Bedford Chapel was built over the site of the conventual church.

The Franciscan Friary, founded in 1240 was suppressed in the same year as the Dominican. The Friars Minors first settled on a plot of ground behind St. Nicholas Priory called Friernhay, now enclosed by Bartholomew Street (quite a near neighbour to South Street). Though the Franciscans embraced poverty and simplicity, the site of the Friary proved too unsanitary even for them; a view endorsed by the Earl of Hereford who lodged there in 1285. After much negotiation the Franciscans moved to a site outside the town walls and the Southgate, west of "Holloway" and near a street still named Friar's Gate. [57] They tapped into springs in the area to provide themselves with a water supply. Successive Bishops authorised the Friars to hear confessions and an Exeter Archdeacon is recorded in 1266 as having granted use of his library to the Friars. [51.2] Much later (1534) and nearer the date of its dissolution, Bishop Hugh Latimer gave a sermon in "the Churchyards of the Grey Ffreers withoute Southgate." The warden of the Friars, one John Cardmaker was enthused by Latimer's preaching, became a keen supporter of the Reformation, was convicted of heresy and was burnt at the stake at Smithfield in 1555. Grey Friars was dissolved in 1538, surrendering to the King's Visitor very modest possessions and heavy debt, so that the Visitor had to pay out more than he acquired to leave the estate solvent. [69]

The monastic house of greatest significance to Sacred Heart parishioners is of course the Priory of St. Nicholas, a Benedictine House founded probably in the 1080s. [29, 33.1, 50.1, 83.1] The other monastic house familiar to Sacred Heart parishioners is Buckfast Abbey, founded in 1018, suppressed in 1539 and re-consecrated in 1932. [52] It is now a flourishing centre of pilgrimage, meetings and tourism. St. Nicholas Priory grew out of the church of St. Olave. When William the Conqueror entered Exeter he granted to the monks of Battle Abbey (Sussex) the church of St. Olave and its properties. The priory of St. Nicholas was built on this ground. The monks followed the famous Rule of St. Benedict with its provision for an ordered life of prayer, labour, study and rest in the Lord's service. [39] Tavistock stood out among Devon Benedictine houses and as already noted, the Bear Inn was an establishment in Exeter of the Abbots of Tavistock. Their range of houses even extended for a time to another St. Nicholas priory in Tresco, Isles of Scilly. [51.2]

St. Nicholas Priory soon attracted grants and bequests which made it virtually independent of its mother abbey at Battle to whom it had to pay a yearly tribute. There is a record of some tension between the monks and the Cathedral chapter, for example in 1103 over the ringing of bells, and of tension between the Priory and the municipality over the rights to the product of Fairs and of fines for misdeeds. [33.1]

The Priory, like the monastic houses throughout the land, provided charity and shelter for the needy. George Oliver quotes from Hooker a specific account of the provisions made at St. Nicholas Priory to provide bread, ale, "flesh" and fish to those in need. It may also have been a source of basic medical treatment. [50.1, 69]

One justification for ending this chapter in 1536 rather than say in 1601 may be quoted from Snell's study of religious foundations in Devon and Cornwall. [69] "In the course of three years (from the Act of Suppression in 1536) was expunged from the face of England one of the greatest and most ancient of her institutions. It was monks who had evangelized England, whether from Rome or from Iona. It was monks who kept scholarship alive in the Dark Ages, who had established the earliest schools, who had provided hospitality for the traveller and the pilgrim, who had fed the poor and nursed the sick. Now by the rapacity of a king and the subservience of Parliament the whole thing was brought to an end, the monastic lands were transferred to lay owners, and the monastic lands sank into decay and ruin, a useful quarry for farmers who wanted good stone to build their barns and fences." Snell points out that the Church of England gained over the whole realm very little from the dissolution - in all, six new bishoprics, poorly endowed.

The Franciscan friary in Exeter with ten friars was surrendered in September 1538 and that of the Black Friars with a community of fifteen on the same day. Inventories of all their possessions were compiled and furnished to the Visitor who passed them on to the Mayor and the receiver for the King. [69] St. Nicholas Priory was suppressed earlier - on September 18th 1536. Hooker's history records the militant opposition by a band of local women to the suppression of what was evidently a much appreciated local social institution. These "certain wives and women of the city" pelted with stones the man sent to demolish the rood screen, so that he had to leap out of a window, and sustained serious injuries. The Mayor of Exeter had to intervene to restore order. The women were released from custody at the intercession of the royal visitors. [33.1, 69]

The monastic foundations were, therefore, not separate from the life of the area in which they were founded, but significant social, as well as religious, institutions. One other Exeter Foundation founded by 1220 is an outstanding example of such an institution. That is the Hospital of St. John, dissolved in 1540, which served to educate as boarders twelve poor persons and eight children. Clearly the suppression of these three institutions alone would have thrown greater burdens onto parishes.

The Elizabethan Poor Law Act of 1601 was a recognition of the need to establish a statutory system (however inadequate) to succeed the combination of parish and monastic provision of the universal church which had operated for centuries previously.

Fig 7 *Sacred Heart Church, The Presbytery, Cathedral Tower, Baptist Church*
[Tegwyn Harris]

We end this chapter with a note on the case of the Bracton Bell. Henry de Bracton, born in Bratton Fleming, an Exmoor village on the Somerset border, was installed as Chancellor of Exeter Cathedral in the year 1264. He became recognised as the most eminent English lawyer of his day. [33.2] The University of Exeter today names the occupant of the chair in the faculty of law as the Bracton Professor. On his death in 1268 Bracton made provision for a chantry mass to be celebrated for the repose of his soul. [37] *

Bendall comments that "a bell was rung every day before this mass was

---

* In referring to this Chancellor, contemporary recorders and later historians seem to use somewhat indiscriminately the names Bracton, de Bracton and Bratton. I have found two monographs helpful in this matter: Samuel E. Thorne, Henry de Bracton, Exeter University Press, 1970 and Lady Radford, Henry de Bracton: a plea for remembrance, Transactions of the Devonshire Association, 1922. Maitland declares categorically "One thing is clear: his name was not Bracton, but Henry of Bratton." (Introduction to <u>Laws & Customs of England</u>, 1807)

celebrated" [P.8] and moreover that in 1964 "that same bell is rung to this day…and is still known as Bracton's Bell." [P.8] This account is replicated in Leaper and McWilliam published in 1984. [41.3] As the present Cathedral virgirs confessed to no knowledge of any such bell - over the past 30 years at any rate - I raised the matter with Reverend Canon Neil Collings, the Acting Dean in 2005. Further advice was given by the Reverend Prebendary John Scott who kindly undertook most meticulous enquiries, consulting the Cathedral Fabric Rolls and other documentation. Prebendary Scott concludes his investigation in these words: "There certainly was a bell named Bracton which no doubt was given by or in memory of Henry Bratton, and there seems to have been a daily requiem mass said for him at his chantry altar, but whether the bell was rung for this mass is not by any means certain. I can't remember hearing of bells being rung for chantry masses, but I'm sure that one would have been rung from the earliest days of the Cathedral before the Capitular Mass, and I would have thought that it was this, rather than a possible ringing for Bratton's requiem, which has continued to the present day."

There the matter rests. It is, however, a reminder of the custom of masses for the dead, which feature prominently among daily dedications (especially during the month of November) in Sacred Heart Church, Exeter, and indeed elsewhere. The "special intentions" of week-day masses are requested by parishioners and are supported by an offering, a large percentage of the masses being intended "for the repose of the soul" of a designated person. As for the bell ringing, the single bell of Sacred Heart Church is rung on Sundays at the consecration during mass, and on a few other special occasions during the year. From Exeter Cathedral the peal of thirteen bells, plus the great clock bell, Peter, ring out with regular frequency. [24, 37]

CHAPTER 4

<u>Christians in Exeter: 1535 - 1792</u>

In the north aisle of Sacred Heart Church, just below the St. Boniface altar, there is on a plinth a small statue of St. Thomas More. It has been admired by many visitors to the church. Occasionally members of the legal profession place flowers in front of it.

Thomas More (1478 - 1535) was a distinguished lawyer, prolific writer, intimate of king and courtiers, who rose to be Chancellor of England. He succeeded Cardinal Thomas Wolsey in that post in 1529 when Wolsey failed to obtain the Pope's agreement to Henry VIII's divorce from Catherine of Aragon. More published works against what he saw as the heretical writings of Tyndale and the declarations of Martin Luther. He supported and advised Henry VIII, whom Pope Leo X had named as Defender of the Faith (Defensor Fidei) in 1521. [31, 38, 64]

In Catholic experience the name of Thomas More has long been linked with that of Bishop John Fisher. Both were distinguished in affairs of church and state; they co-operated in published writings against Lutheranism. John Fisher, Bishop of Rochester, was instrumental in the foundation of St. John's College, Cambridge and by 1501 was appointed Vice-Chancellor of Cambridge University. [38,44,59]

As a result of their refusal to recognise the king as head of the Church of England both were sentenced to be beheaded by the King's command on Tower Hill in 1535. Four hundred years later More and Fisher were both proclaimed saints by the Pope in 1935, after re-iterated petitions from Catholics in England, including parishioners of Sacred Heart, Exeter. [31]

Thomas More's life has been the subject of revived interest among Sacred Heart parishioners - and of course very many others - in recent years: in a long-running play, a television programme and a widely-read biography published in 1998.[*] Thomas More "who died the King's good servant, but God's first" was, according to Ackroyd, not only a saintly, learned and original man, but also a man of contemporary culture. He did approve of the burning of heretics. One of these was Thomas Benet, burnt for heresy in Exeter in the fifteen thirties. [51.2]

In Paris in the year before the Tower Hill executions of Saints More and Fisher, there was founded by St. Ignatius Loyola and a few followers the Society of

---

[*] The most recent and authoritative work (among very many biographical studies) is: Ackroyd, Peter: The Life of Thomas More, Chatto & Windus, 1998. It contains an extensive bibliography.

Jesus. [28] The Jesuits were to be instrumental in the revival of the Roman Catholic faith in England and in particular in Exeter. [P.3, 29, 40,54] The events in London in 1535 were to have other powerful influences on the relations of church and state, some of which have persisted to this day. [51.2, 80]

It seems hard to assess from contemporary records the immediate effect of the execution at the King's command of two leading figures in church and state upon priests and laity in local parishes of the church. What also was the effect of the persecution - and execution - of so many in the reigns of Edward, Mary and Elizabeth?

Devon in the mid sixteenth century has been described as "solidly traditional in religion as in everything else." [23.1] The Lollards earlier and the declarations of Martin Luther at the time seem to have received very little support. [23.2] In 1531 there was the case of Thomas Benet who posted anti-Papal notices on the door of Exeter Cathedral. His story is chronicled by the historian John Hooker. He was found guilty of heresy and burnt at the stake at Livery Dole to the east of the city, close to the modern site of Blessed Sacrament, Heavitree Catholic Church. [51.2] Bishop Veysey of Exeter Diocese seems to have acquiesced in King Henry's actions, including his being declared head of the Church of England in 1534. [23.1] In 1537, a convinced Protestant reformer, Dr. Simon Heynes, was appointed Dean of the Cathedral. He argued for a reduction in the liturgical vestments and images and an increase in allocations to schools and care of the poor. [23.1] However, Heynes was so unpopular in Exeter that he left, and by 1543 found himself heavily fined by the Privy Council for "lewde and seditious preaching." [23.1] Veysey's successor, however, was Bishop James Tuberville who resisted King Henry's Reformation, was deprived of his see, imprisoned in the Tower of London for three years, and died in 1570 after his release. Bishop Tuberville is commemorated in a painting on canvas now on the south wall of the sanctuary of Sacred Heart Church.

Many citizens of Exeter, as well as members of distinguished families in the big houses of surrounding Devon, made their accommodation with the new church governance, though often at sacrifice to themselves. [51.2] George Oliver was to record later that many local Exeter citizens profited from the change of ownership of monastic buildings. [50.3] For example, the sovereign had granted to Sir Thomas Denys the buildings of St. Nicholas Priory in 1540, which Sir Thomas sold to Exeter Corporation. "Such was the barbarous taste of the new proprietors," wrote Oliver, "that they demolished the venerable structure of St. Nicholas Church, the ornament of the city, and the admiration of strangers, for the miserable purpose of getting material to patch up the town walls and to stop up gaps in Exeter bridge." However, from other evidence we learn that St. Nicholas Priory Church was dismantled immediately after the Dissolution, probably by order of the Crown Commissioners. [69]

Snell [69] records that a number of ex-religious in Devon and Cornwall, displaced from religious houses, were given pensions, and augmented those pensions by finding employment as chantry priests, chaplains to wealthy families, prebendaries and incumbents of parochial livings. For example, Richard Harrys, prior of the Hospital of St. John, Exeter was presented to the Vicarage of Brampford Speke.

Bishop Charles Graham in an ms. history of Plymouth diocese wrote in 1911 that "Catholic families resident here bought liberty for the practice of their religion by 'compositions' or by suffering forfeits and sequestrations of their lands and means." [29] Graham cites the fate of the Courtenays of Powderham Castle. The story of the Clifford family of Chudleigh is different. Though requesting the Anglican Bishop Anthony Sparrow (1667-76) to consecrate the chapel at Ugbrooke, Sir Thomas Clifford was a Catholic and was involved with Charles II in the secret treaty of Dover.* (We shall see the role of a Clifford in providing essential support for the building of Sacred Heart Church in a later century). Ugbrooke had been church land for centuries, being once occupied by the Precentor to the Bishop of Exeter. It is in 2004 a place of frequent Catholic visitation, and Mass is said there on Sundays and Holy Days of Obligation by the priest living in Bovey Tracey. What a good example of change and continuity! [P.4]

Reviewing the rapid and contradictory changes made under successive Tudor monarchs Nicholas Orme concludes: "These changes were received by most of the parish clergy and their parishioners without resistance... Sometimes the churches took a little time to respond to changes, but it is difficult to know if the reason was a positive dislike of them or mere laziness and inefficiency. It was dangerous to oppose the changes in public and rare to comment on them in church records." [51.2] Simon Schama comments in detail in his history of the struggle between Henry VIII and the Papacy [65] on the "grovelling submission" of the large majority of the clergy (in contrast to the stand taken by Saints John Fisher and Thomas More). Moreover no core doctrines of the church had been touched, the King had got his divorce, Anne Boleyn had been crowned in Westminster Abbey, and interference with the traditional church might have stopped there. In Schama's interpretation the changes which did come about, and which resulted in fierce struggles and hostility, were due far more to the political maneuverings of Thomas Cranmer and Thomas Cromwell. Certainly the political and the religious were interwoven under Queen Elizabeth's reign.

Hoskins reminds us that we can still see a good deal of the continuity of the city of Exeter merely by looking at the medieval buildings still standing - despite depredations due to religious conflict, civil war, and bombardment in 1942. "It is not so much the buildings," wrote Hoskins, "but what went on within them that aroused the ire and the opposition of the majority who would have liked things to stay more or less as they were." [33.1]

---

* The story of this "Treaty" is recounted in "Henrietta of Exeter" by T.W.E. Roche, Phillimore, 1971. Her portrait by Sir Peter Lely hangs in Exeter Guildhall. She died in France in 1670.

"What went on within the churches" certainly gave rise to a well-chronicled event in 1549 which brought armed rebels to the walls of Exeter City. It was provoked by the enforced use of the Book of Common Prayer, but it seems to have had political undertones which became more evident as events progressed. This was what has come to be known as the Prayer Book Rebellion. [51.2] The imposition of the new order of service had provoked rebellion elsewhere in England, notably in the Pilgrimage of Grace in the north, and in Bodmin in Cornwall, while the story of the obduracy of Morebath parish is vividly described in Professor Eamon Duffy's study. [21.1]

Fig 8   The Banner of "The Five Wounds" - 1549 Prayer Book Rising

The Prayer Book Rebellion started with a fracas in the country parish of Sampford Courtenay, a few miles from Exeter. The parishioners had refused the orders of the King's Council that the new Book of Common Prayer be used and had gone back to the Latin Mass. The rebels asserted that "We will not receive the new service because it is like a Christmas game, but we will have our old service of the Mass in Latin as it was before... every priest in his Mass shall pray especially by name for the souls in Purgatory as our forefathers did." [23.1] The rebels' demands included some political and social objectives, including a limitation on the number of servants kept by the gentry. "They wanted holders of monastic lands to give back half to re-establish two abbeys in each county (Devon and Cornwall)." [51.2] They wanted to re-establish relations with Rome, to be ensured of the recall of Cardinal Pole who had been deposed as Dean of Exeter in 1537 when the actively Protestant Simon Heynes had replaced him. Within a month of the clashes at Sampford Courtenay a peasant army of several thousand and involving people from a wide range of villages in Devon and Cornwall marched on Exeter and set up camps in a ring around the city, including one in Southernhay down to the Westgate. It was reported that the rebels burnt copies of the Book of Common Prayer in their camps. [23.1]

Lord Russel, the Lord Privy Seal, was dispatched to put down the rebellion, but encountered hostility and a lack of will on the part even of the gentry to defeat the "rank rebels and papists of Devon." Eventually re-inforced by foreign mercenaries, Russel defeated the rebels in a bloody battle at Clyst St. Mary. The besiegers of the City melted away, their remnants being pursued across the Devon and Cornwall countryside. It is estimated that 4,000 rebels were killed in the rebellion whose perpetrators were pursued with ruthlessness. [23.1] The vicar of St. Thomas Church, Robert Welshe, who had sympathised with the rebels and was known as a devout Catholic, rejecting the use of the Prayer Book, was treated brutally. Lord Russel condemned him to be hung in chains, dressed in his priestly apparel, from the tower of St. Thomas Church until he died from exposure. The historian John Hooker gave an account of Welshe's suffering and death. [23.1] Today the Rebellion is commemorated in Sacred Heart Church by a large banner replicating that carried by the rebels.

Was the Prayer Book Rebellion a protest against changes in forms of religious observance or was that a pretext for an uprising against the forces of economic and social change involved in the Reformation? Professor Joyce Youings remains sceptical of the religious observance explanation, but Professor Eamon Duffy argues that in Tudor England it would have been impossible to separate "religious causes" from social and economic structures. [23.2]

The abolition of Holy Days by Cromwell's Act of Convocation (1536) had a professed economic purpose - to improve productivity. It was a widely unpopular action since it abolished, or certainly discouraged, major local events like fairs and markets. Cromwell's injunction to the clergy required parents and employers to ensure that children and servants learnt their prayers in English, not Latin; the same injunctions urged that the cult of images and pilgrimages be abandoned and the money saved given to the poor and needy. [23.1]

Under the Protectorship of Somerset, King Edward's Parliament extended Protestant influence; the Second Prayer Book was introduced in 1552 and Thomas Cranmer promulgated the Forty-two articles of faith in the following year. [23.1] The Council of Trent in 1551 had affirmed the doctrine of *transubstantiation*, declaring that "by the consecration of bread and wine there takes place a change of the whole substance of the bread into the substance of the body of Christ Our Lord, and of the whole substance of the wine into the substance of His blood. This change the Holy Catholic Church has fittingly and properly called *transubstantiation*." [36.1] This may

be contrasted with Article 28 of the 39 Articles of 1562, where it is declared:
"Transubstantiation (or the change of the substance of Bread and Wine) in the
Supper of the Lord, cannot be proved by Holy Writ; but is repugnant to the plain
words of Scripture, overthroweth the nature of a Sacrament, and hath given occasion
to many superstitions. The Body of Christ is given, taken and eaten in the Supper,
only after a heavenly and spiritual manner." [*]

Despite the many ways in which continuity of worship seemed assured, there were
clear differences between the practices prevalent under Henry VIII and those which
became general under the reigns of his offspring. When Queen Mary began her short
reign in 1553 (marrying Philip of Spain in the following year) she was instrumental
in repealing the legislation passed during Edward's reign about the Prayer Book,
sacred images and married priests. The 1555 Act of Repeal re-united England with
Rome. Mary is on record, however, as bidding Cardinal Pole to exercise caution in
seeking to re-establish Catholic worship, [51.2] and to recognise the standing of
Parliament and the English ecclesiastical courts. Locally in Exeter the Catholic
mayor, Walter Steplehill, was tolerant of the Protestant element in the city, as seems
to have been the case elsewhere in Devon. [33.3] The records of the parish of
Morebath in North Devon show that the vicar and wardens presented to the diocesan
office in Exeter an inventory of what was needed to restore the Catholic liturgy in a
country parish. [23.1] Much the same process is recorded for the (hitherto reformed)
Exeter City parish of St. Petrock's. During Mary's reign, therefore the Catholic
tendency was legitimised and patriotic, whereas at other times Catholics were
identified by their enemies as agents of foreign interests. Given that Catholics were,
under Elizabeth and later, obliged to set up Catholic centres abroad and to re-enter
their country secretly under pain of death, some credibility could easily be given to
such Papist stereotypes. [38] Queen Mary's reign was disfigured in Exeter by the
burning at the stake in Southernhay of Agnes Prest convicted of heresy in 1558. The
Barnfield Road-Denmark Road martyrs' memorial in Exeter commemorates other
victims. [42] Elsewhere heretics continued to be burnt at the stake, notably Latimer
and Ridley outside Balliol College, Oxford in 1555. Thomas Cranmer's appeal to
the Papal General Council having failed, he suffered the same fate. We can only
guess at what would have happened had Mary's reign been prolonged, and we have
very little evidence of its local effects in Exeter. However, both the Queen and
Cardinal Pole died in London on the same day in 1558. Queen Elizabeth came to the
throne in that same year. She was crowned in the following January at a Mass sung
by the Dean of the Queen's Chapel, partly in Latin and partly in English. [38]

New legislation in the Elizabethan era effected the supremacy of the monarch over
the church, and enforced uniformity with the Book of Common Prayer under pain of
fines or imprisonment. [38] Despite strong opposition from Convocation, forwarded
to Parliament, moves were made to promote a Westminster Conference at which
Protestant Bishops (some recently returned from abroad after Mary's rule) disputed

---

[*] The 39 Articles of Religion are appended to the Book of Common Prayer.

with those holding the traditional Catholic doctrines of transubstantiation and the use of Latin instead of the vernacular at church services. The Conference was dissolved without conclusion and most of the Catholic disputants were either dismissed or imprisoned. [38, 80]

Pope Pius V proceeded in 1570 to excommunicate Queen Elizabeth for having "unnaturally usurped to herself the place of supreme head of the church in England." To this was added having oppressed those continuing to observe Catholic practice, of having imprisoned bishops, rectors and others, and of having given their benefices to heretics. The old hierarchy in place when Elizabeth came to the throne was soon extinct and the break with Rome was complete, at least at national level.

In 1599 the Venerable James Dowdall was convicted of denying the Queen's spiritual supremacy and was hanged, drawn and quartered at Exeter Castle. Records show that several martyrs were kept in the old Devon County Gaol before execution, and other Roman Catholics were detained there for long periods. [79]

In 1559, Queen Elizabeth's visitors are recorded by John Hooker as having "defaced, pulled downe and burned all the statues and images in Exeter Cathedral." [24] Many of them had been re-installed in Mary's reign. What seems to have emerged under the "Elizabethan Settlement" was a mixed national church, conscious of external threats and willing to accept reform. The Church under James I and Charles I, Elizabeth's successors, was under threat of fragmentation from within and later on of threats from Jacobite Catholicism from without. Jonathan Barry writes that "there are dangers in offering an account of church history too rooted in the denominational divisions which had resulted by the nineteenth century." In reviewing the history of one parish in Exeter we must be acutely aware of such a danger in the twenty-first century, especially as our *local* written evidence is sparse. [51.2]

To many of us in 2005 it may seem hard to avoid two conflicting emotions as we read of the brutal tortures and executions of the sixteenth century. The first is a feeling of reverent admiration for the martyrs who were steadfast in their faith unto death, whatever the cause they espoused. The second is one of revulsion at the brutality of the tortures and killings carried out. It seems too simplistic to dismiss them as "part of the culture of the time." [31, 47, 79]

In October, 1970 Pope Paul VI canonised forty martyrs of England and Wales; eighty-five candidates having been proposed for beatification. In Sacred Heart Church, Exeter, Bishop Cyril Restieaux was the principal celebrant at Mass to commemorate the canonisations. Part of the skull of Saint Cuthbert Mayne was venerated. [P.1] Cuthbert Mayne was born near Barnstaple and in adult life was convicted of entering England from the English College in Douai and of promulgating Papal material. He was hanged, drawn and quartered at Launceston in 1577. Many parishioners from Exeter have taken part in pilgrimages to Launceston over the years. During the preparation of the cause for the beatification of eighty-five candidates for submission to Rome, the Catholic hierarchy held prudent consultations with the British Council of Churches. The Council issued a statement to the effect that: "The martyr tradition is one which all have shared and from which all may draw strength, even across denominational boundaries." The Archbishop of Canterbury stated "I hope with Cardinal Hume that the beatification of the eighty-five martyrs will indeed prompt all the Christians of England, Wales and Scotland to pursue the path of reconciliation and reunion with greater understanding and effectiveness." [P.10]

The dramatic changes of the sixteenth century emphasised the way in which forms of worship determine both the structure and the furnishing of churches. As Simon Jenkins puts it: "A church is primarily a theatre for its liturgy." [*] After the promulgation of the Book of Common Prayer daily services were altered, the parish church nave became the focus of activity, side aisles and chantries (where they existed) were no longer needed or were put to other uses, rood screens were destroyed as redolent of services separate from the people conducted by a clerical elite. As already noted, the attempt to take down the rood screen from St. Nicholas Priory led to physical conflict between workmen employed by the Reformers and women of the local parish. [1, 33.3] At Sacred Heart Church we have a vestigial (and impressive) rood screen in wrought iron - an interesting nineteenth century sign of continuity in church furnishing. The Eastern Orthodox Church emphasises in its architecture the sacredness of the Eucharist by building and maintaining the screen between nave and chancel. The English Congregational tradition on the other hand built and maintained churches with a focus on the pulpit, thus emphasising the preaching of the Word and participation in worship. Further examples are the changing use of: the baptismal font, altar rails, sedilia and piscina. [38, 58, 80]

By the 1600s several historians record a marked decline in the number of Roman Catholics in Devon compared to those of fifty years earlier - though estimates vary. [51.2] Belloc hazards an informed guess of a gradual reduction in England during the seventeenth century from a third to an eighth of the population. George Oliver traces [50.2] a sharp reduction in Devon due to the variable factors of persecution, accommodation or the influence of powerful families. The latter seems to have been a decisive factor with Catholic gentry in the Exeter area and also for example in a remote parish like Molland in North Devon. Here Catholic lords of the manor (the recusant Courtenay family originally) had little interest in the local parish church whose furnishings were left unmolested and which is also an excellent example of the importance of the pulpit in a Protestant church with its three-tier structure surmounted by a large tester. Sacred Heart Church in Exeter focussed attention on its pulpit when it was first built and at one stage erected a tester above it. What changing use is to be found for the pulpit in the twenty-first century?

---

[*] References to Simon Jenkins are from his "England's Thousand Best Churches," Penguin, 2000.

James I ascended the throne of England in 1603, having been James VI of Scotland since 1567 on the abdication of his mother, Mary Queen of Scots. She was executed by Elizabeth in 1587. James seemed at first to signal toleration for Roman Catholics, but in 1606 called on all of them to take the Oath of Allegiance. Only two years after his anointing as King the Gunpowder Plot was foiled. [38] It provided a focal point for anti-Popish demonstrations, including bonfires outside the West front of Exeter Cathedral, for about two hundred years. It lost its religious and political significance in the twentieth century and many Sacred Heart parishioners (and especially their children) nowadays participate in the November 5th firework and bonfire night ritual party.

King James I had enacted a requirement for all Catholics to take an oath of allegiance to the Crown; it was met with blank refusal by many - especially the Jesuit missionaries, supported by the Papacy. In an endeavour to restore relations with Catholics in England several methods were tried out. Cardinal William Allan, prominent at Oxford University under both Mary and Elizabeth, left for Flanders in 1561 and became head of the seminary at Douai which trained many English missionaries, including Cuthbert Mayne. Allan became Papal representative to England although unable to assume his full duties here. [38] The device then tried was that of appointing an "arch-priest" of whom there were three. The expressed wish of many Catholic laity and clergy was for a new Bishop. Instead of this, "vicars apostolic" were appointed which provoked strong opposition from King and Anglican Church but eventually went ahead. The "vicar apostolic" of the Western District (which covered Exeter) was Philip Ellis OSB, whose Benedictine name was Michael. [P.4, P.8]

King Charles I's quarrels with Parliament culminated in the Civil War, which destroyed much of the country and broke the unity of crown and church for the first time since Henry VIII. The upheaval, characterised by Hilaire Belloc as "The Great Rebellion" clearly had a variety of deadly ingredients: political, civil, military and religious. [33.3, 38, 51.2] In the struggle "the King was supported throughout by the large Catholic body, which the much larger Protestant numbers of the nation now hated." The land-owners were divided in their allegiance to King or Parliament, but the Catholic minority among them did support the King, notably the Marquis of Worcester. Queen Henrietta Maria took refuge in Exeter in June 1644 and gave birth to her child here, an event commemorated by her portrait in Exeter Guildhall. The Queen escaped to France in a Dutch boat via Plymouth. There in Paris she was to learn of the London execution of Charles I in 1649.

Exeter was involved in many ways in the Civil War, and feelings and allegiances were divided and changeable, not necessarily following class divisions. The Dean and Chapter of Exeter Cathedral were unequivocally Royalist as were many of the leading merchants, but there were also parliamentarians in the city. Hoskins gives a vivid account of the two sieges of the city, and the stout city wall defences, both in 1643 (when the Royalists triumphed) and in 1645-6 (when the Royalist garrison surrendered to Sir Thomas Fairfax). Parliamentary soldiers under John Disbrowe,

Cromwell's brother-in-law, now occupied the city until the Restoration of the monarchy under Charles II.

When the Protectorate was established in 1653 and a parliament was elected on a very limited franchise, it included Thomas Bampfylde, recorder of Exeter, living at Poltimore. The "parliament" did not last long. John Disbrowe's defence of Exeter in 1655 against a Royalist up-rising led by John Penruddock, captured and executed, caused far more local stir. It also led to a system of tax upon known and suspected royalists which had to be dropped due to the unpopularity always attached to local government taxation, now and then. The Cromwellian regime seems, however, to have been "moderately tolerant in religion, too tolerant for some even of its own government." Arthur Gabb's local history of the Baptist Church in Exeter (immediately adjacent to Sacred Heart Church) [11] gives the probable date of its foundation as 1649, the Cathedral Deanery Hall having been used as their meeting place before that. From 1654 Quakers began to spread in the city, despite being periodically fined or imprisoned for meeting to worship. The death of Oliver Cromwell and the proclamation of Richard as Protector was followed by street disorders in Exeter in 1659, and eventually to the Restoration of the monarchy under Charles II proclaimed at three places in Exeter. By that time Exeter's damaged trade was recovering well, [33.3] especially its woollen industries. The Custom House on the Quay was built in 1681, a sure sign of export and import business and of renewed activity in the area around South Street and down to the River Exe. Overcrowded houses and dangerous building materials led to serious plague outbreaks and the city centre fires in the 60s and 70s. Ivan Roots concludes his short review of the Commonwealth and Restoration with the comment "Devon was going through an age of transition, one of both change and continuity (which is a sort of linear change). It was a time perhaps even more than under Elizabeth I, when the county and its people were energetic, curious and interested in natural developments with which their own history was intertwined." [61]

Since 1657 a large wall had been erected across the pulpitum screen in Exeter Cathedral to provide for separately worshipping congregations of Presbyterians and Independents. The dean and chapter's control of the Cathedral had been removed from them by Ordinance of the House of Commons in 1649, and the Puritan city chamber was given control. The wall was demolished in 1660; several other alterations were being made to the Cathedral at the time. These included provisions for a new serge market right against the Cathedral cloister garth because the old one in South Street was open to the elements. [51.1] The return of the monarchy in 1660 ushered in a new era for the Cathedral and for the parishes of Exeter. This included the installation of the 1665 Loosemore organ in the Cathedral. For Catholics the outlook was less rosy; a reference in a document about Bishop Ward of Exeter claims that the Restoration gave hope of "a general toleration of all religions, *excepting Popery...*" [24] Nevertheless Charles II formed a policy of friendship with Louis XIV of France, even to signing a secret treaty with him. Thomas Clifford of Ugbrooke was instrumental in these negotiations and was known to be a Catholic. At this time an estimate of the number of recusants in Devon is 250, including the

Chichesters of Arlington Court. When the conversion to Catholicism of the future James II became known anti-papist laws were passed - the 1673 and 1678 Test Acts. The mayor of Exeter, standing for parliamentary election in 1679 was attacked for being a Papist. When James II succeeded in 1685 he had to face a revolt by the Duke of Monmouth, eldest illegitimate son of Charles II who claimed loyalty to Protestantism. After his army's defeat at Sedgemoor the rebels were dealt with harshly, some 300 being executed in Exeter alone. James offered two Declarations of Indulgence to recusants, and they were to be read out in all churches. Oliver comments "a gleam of sunshine and toleration appeared during the short reign of James II."

A chapel, called a "Mass House" was built at this time, but it was "completely demolished at the Revolutionary explosion," [50.3] and George Oliver was not able to trace its site. It was being served by a Jesuit priest, Fr. Richard Morris, who narrowly escaped with his life. After that, Exeter's Roman Catholic group was served by occasional visiting priests. The news of the birth of a royal son was greeted with some alarm, especially in London's political circles where it opened the prospect of a king openly favourable to Roman Catholics. King James' manoeuvering at the end of his short reign included moves to give greater freedom of worship to all his subjects, but his adherence to the Catholic faith cost him his throne. William of Orange, firmly Protestant and married to James' daughter Mary, recruited naval and military support and landed at Brixham in 1688. Having marched to Exeter he rode up Stepcote Hill and stayed twelve nights in Exeter Deanery (uncertain of the reception he would have) before going on to London. The "Glorious Revolution" meant a fairly peaceful transition to a joint monarchy and a firmly re-established national church, together with a florescence of Nonconformist groups. [38] The Toleration Act of 1689 gave authorisation for Nonconformist worship in licensed chapels. Their governance and financing in Exeter, for example, was of a markedly different model to the system of the Anglican parish church. In the same year, however, 1689 an Act of Parliament excluded from the throne anyone who was a Catholic or married to a Catholic. This provision remains valid, though under review in the twenty first century.

Roman Catholics still suffered under serious social and political disabilities. They assumed aliases, wrote in code to evade persecution, worshipped in secret and were subject to periodic outbreaks of violence. George Oliver wrote "We hardly met with a priest but in the state of a prisoner." [50.3] There is good evidence that Catholic prelates favoured the Stuarts and the great poet, John Dryden, wrote and published his long poem in defence of the Catholic Church in 1687. Later in the eighteenth century the two Jacobite risings of 1715 and 1745 caused hostility to Catholics in England, though Bishop Stonor, Vicar Apostolic of the Midland District, sought to distance himself and the Catholic cause from the Jacobites and to accept the Hanoverians - but in this he was opposed by Bishop Griffard and the majority of Catholic leaders. [38]

At the bottom of the north aisle in Sacred Heart Church are stained glass windows installed to commemorate the golden jubilee of the opening of the church (See Chapter 1). It was in 1673 that St. Margaret-Mary Alacoque first made known her apparitions in which Our Lord told her his wish for special honour to be paid to his Sacred Heart, particularly by Holy Communion on the first Friday of each month and a special act of reparation offered on the Friday within the Octave of Corpus Christi. It is often forgotten that devotion to the Sacred Heart, so widespread in the nineteenth and twentieth centuries in England, was initiated only five years after the arrival of William and Mary and the flight of James II. [10]

James was established in exile in France from where he was a continuing menace. In 1689 James landed in Ireland, to be opposed in person by William at a battle with political and religious resonance ever since - the Battle of the Boyne. The wars with France spilled over from William and Mary's to Queen Anne's reign where Marlborough's ascendancy was ubiquitous. The Treaty of Utrecht in 1713 marked the end of the ten years of wars with France over the Spanish Succession.

A considerable debt is owed by our forefathers in the early eighteenth century, and by their descendants, to the best known of the Vicars Apostolic, namely Bishop Richard Challonor. After work at the Douai Seminary he returned to the London district, first as auxiliary to Bishop Petre and then in 1758 as Vicar Apostolic. He was a prolific writer, translator, and historian of Catholic martyrs; starting with Blessed Cuthbert Mayne. Challonor's revised translation of the Bible is an interesting combination of the Douay version and of the Authorised version; his works were widely used by the remaining Catholics in England. [38]

During this period, according to a note by George Oliver, [P.3] "an old man, John Flood, who was born in Exeter 16th Feb. 1724 and died at the age of 91, said that the service (ie: Mass) was performed in an upper room of Mr. Flashman's house, commonly called King John's Entry, in South Street." He goes on to name three priests: a Franciscan, a Benedictine and "a secular clergyman" who performed the services. This account is repeated in Bishop Graham's later MS in which he adds that the work in South Street went on "till at least 1756." After service by a number of Jesuits, with the approval of Bishop Walmesley of the Western District, the Rev. John Edisford S.J. transferred the Chapel from Flashman's King John's Tavern to Bartholomew Street. [50.4]

The number of Catholics in Devon during the eighteenth century has been variously estimated. [51.2, 43, 33.2] In 1705 it has been stated that there were about 220 and by 1767 it had slightly increased to 235. 1773 Catholic returns available to Kevin MacGrath writing in 1962 show 440 Devon Catholics. Among them were 27 Catholics in Exeter city, including William Gillibrand "a reputed priest." As has been written several times, a great debt is owed for the survival of the Old Faith to the landed families mentioned by MacGrath including: the Cliffords of Chudleigh (Ugbrooke House), the Carys of Torre Abbey, the Rowes of Beaston, the Kirkhams of Newton St. Cyres, the Chichesters of Arlington. These families seem in many ways to have enjoyed friendly relationships with the clergy of the Established Church and indeed five were actually patrons of Anglican parishes (Cf. Molland parish already mentioned). The children of these families tended to be educated in France or Belgium and several of them joined Benedictine or Franciscan convents in Belgium, notably in Brugge at the Prinsenhof. At the French Revolution many were obliged to flee back to England. Contacts between English Catholics and fellow religionists in Ireland, France and Belgium were well maintained, despite the obvious travel problems of the time. [38]

In Exeter in 1775 premises in the Mint were rented from one Mr. Gibbs for the Catholic Incumbant at a cost of £25 per annum. [P.3] They were finally purchased on July 23rd 1788 for £400. Hugh, Lord Clifford allowed his name to go forward as the purchaser and by deed dated 16th Sept. 1799 he disclaimed for himself or his heirs any right to the premises. In effect they were now to be used by the priest and Catholic people of Exeter. The foundation stone of the Catholic chapel was laid in May 1790, and the first Mass was celebrated there on the Feast of the Epiphany, 1792. The chapel had been recorded in the previous year as "A place of religious worship for persons professing the Roman Catholic religion." [51.2] The Reverend George Oliver took the Oath of Allegiance and was recorded as the priest and minister of the Catholic Congregation of Exeter in the Guildhall on the 9th of July 1810. Bishop Walmesley of the Western District is recorded by Bishop Graham as having confirmed 10 people on June 6th, 1793.

In the remarkable "Chapel Book" still in the Sacred Heart Church archives, the Reverend George Oliver has written in his own hand the account of the proceedings of the Committee of Catholic Gentlemen in the city of Exeter copied from notes prepared by one Mr. Halloran, the secretary. This gentleman kept a small school, first in Butcher Row and then in Southernhay. Unfortunately he was convicted of forging a frank of a wealthy citizen and was sentenced to be transported to Australia. He sailed from Sheerness in a convict-ship and later died in Sydney. [P.3]

Nevertheless the committee valiantly pursued its objective. George Oliver records its progress in these extracts from the Chapel Book. He had prepared this account from the records kept by the committee secretary:

> August 19th 1788
>
> It was agreed that a Committee of Gentlemen should be appointed to preside over the undertaking, to manage & direct the expenditure of the public contributions, conformably to the intention of the Donors & interest of the Congregation. ~ On this principle the following Gentlemen having no other object than the public welfare in view with the consent & approbation of the Congregation at large, formed themselves into a Temporary Committee for carrying the above mentioned plan into execution.

<u>Rev. John Edisford</u>
<u>Edward Cary Esq.</u>
<u>Ambrose Ferrall Esq.</u>
<u>Mr. John Couche</u>
<u>Maurice Lyston Esq.</u>
<u>Mr. James Brooke</u>
<u>Mr Wm Smith</u>
<u>Mr L. H. J. Halloran</u>

By this committee thus formed, it was unanimously agreed, that the duty &
design of this Committee is

1. To look out for and fix upon some convenient spot, which shall be purchased
    & appropriated for the purpose of erecting a Public Chapel & commodious
    dwelling house for a Clergyman, who under the authority & jurisdiction of
    the Bishop of the Western District, shall be ready at all times to attend &
    assist the Congregation of Exeter in their spiritual concerns.
2. To meet together when called upon for the dispatch of business & to
    discharge & determine all such matters as shall be proposed to them, for the
    promoting & finishing of the present undertaking.
3. To inspect the accompts and direct the expenditure of the collected monies,
    of which no part shall be disposed of, but by their consent & direction for the
    public good. And when by their zealous & steady exertions, the Gentlemen
    of the Committee shall have executed their plan & put a finishing hand to the
    necessary buildings, it is now agreed that the Committee shall be thought to
    have done the whole & sole work for which it was first instituted & of course,
    that it shall then cease.

These preliminary points being maturely weighed & unanimously approved
of the Committee proceeded to act in consequence thereof - & being duly
furnished with every information they wished for on the subject before them,
they unanimously came to the following resolutions.

Resolved

1, That the Premises now occupied by the Rev. John Edisford in the Mint,
appear to be commodiously situated & more suitable to our purpose than any
other spot to be now met with in the City of Exeter.

2, That the price of £400, at which Mr. Gibbs the Proprietor in Fee, offers the
said Premises to us, seems a reasonable price & not to be refused.

3, That the Title deeds be put into the hands of Mr. Jones who, has the repute
of being an able & judicious Lawyer, to be examined; & if the Title shall by

him be found to be good & sound in law, that the purchase deeds be immediately drawn & prepared for signing with all possible speed.

4, That Mr. Edisford be directed to call in the Subscriptions he has solicited, that the purchase money be paid off & the bargain finally closed as soon as possible.

5, That the thanks of the Committee be given to the Rt. Hon. Lord Clifford for having graciously lent them his name in the purchase – writings & that his Lordship be requested to sign a Deed, declaring the uses & intentions of the said Purchase.

6, That the necessary repairs of the Dwelling-house be immediately done out of hand in order to keep it dry, until sufficient monies are received to answer the expense of a thorough repair.

7, That it is the instruction to each member of the Committee to exert his utmost zeal & interest in procuring subscriptions for the building of the Chapel, which shall begin as soon as a competent sum is subscribed & not before.

Adjourned to Sept.2.1788

Signed by

Joseph Reeve
John Edisford
James Brooke
Ambrose Ferrall
L.H.J. Halloran

George Oliver further notes that on his arrival there on 27th October 1807 he found the chapel in a bad condition. "It was naked of ornament and ill provided with vestmants & C&C. Since that time (including the expense of Mr. Reeve Gallery) the sum spent on repairs and improvements have amounted to nearly £400. Thank God, the chapel and premises are perfectly clear of debt," Sept. 12th 1819.

The Chapel Book conscientiously records the list of subscribers to the funds for "the purchasing of the premises and beautifying the Chapel & C." Between the years 1807 and 1820 forty seven donors are recorded. The amounts of individual donations range from a modest guinea (£1 - 1 - 0) to several contributions of £50. Lord Petre, Sir Robert Throckmorton, Hugh Lord Clifford, Rev. Jos. Reeve, Rev. W. Poole and the Reverend John Edisford himself figure among the largest donors. The largest of all - that of £130 - is credited mysteriously to "Mary the Devout."

The expenditure recorded in the Chapel by the Rev. Jos. Reeve includes an item for a new gallery, for colouring and painting, and for "ventilation etc" amounting to £127.13.0. At Christmas in 1820 Mrs. L. Long paid for "the gilding of 6 large candlesticks." An old ciborium was bought for £1.17.9, and the carving of two wooden candlesticks cost two guineas. In 1821-22 repairing the roof accounts for several small items of expenditure. Eight yards of green cotton was purchased for 10/-6d.

More substantial equipment included an organ which was bought in London at a total cost of a hundred guineas. A Mr. Chadwick was engaged as the chapel organist for £12 per annum. The organ was first played on Christmas Eve in 1826 when "Mr. and Mrs. Caddell sang the Alma Redemptoris, the Adeste Fideles and Tantum Ergo."

To avoid confusion it should be noted that references to the "dwelling house" or "the cottage" or the "priests' house" all appear to relate to the same edifice, namely 21, The Mint. Later developments to this building and to the Mint Catholic chapel, are described in a later chapter. George Oliver particularly asked for an Annual Mass to be celebrated for the pioneers who worked so hard to establish the Chapel and the priests' house, and who attended Mass and other services there in the early years.

So, by the year 1792 Mass was celebrated in an established Exeter chapel for the first time since the Reformation. It was the beginning of a new era for Catholics in Exeter, and for their relations with other Christians in the city.

CHAPTER 5

<u>From Mint to South Street: The Nineteenth Century</u>

This chapter covers the development of Sacred Heart Parish and is a good deal shorter than the last. However, it is a period of dramatic growth in the parish, which has to be set in the context of striking change in the affairs of church and state, both locally and nationally - firstly during what has been dubbed "the Georgian Age." [11] By Royal Command a census of religious observance was taken in 1767. It covered Papists, of whom only 28 were recorded in Exeter, including the visiting Jesuit priest who ministered to this tiny congregation. Included also was one "Mr. Searle" who kept the Bear Inn, on part of the ground now occupied by the Sacred Heart Church.[43] Here visiting priests were recorded as staying on their visits, until the premises first in Bartholomew Street and then in the Mint were rented, and then purchased, for clergy use. Fr. John Edisford, appointed by Bishop Charles Walmsley OSB in 1772, worked until he died in 1789, having caught fever from his visits to prisoners in Exeter prison, then in the South Gate, described by Hoskins as "one of the foulest holes in England." [33.3]

The Mint Chapel immediately adjacent to the remains of St. Nicholas Priory was officially recorded as a place of religious worship for Roman Catholics in 1791. The Reverend William Poole succeeded John Edisford as priest. Despite the paucity of the initial congregation, there had been two vocations to the priesthood, both mentioned in the 1964 "Story of Catholic Exeter" as being of the family name of Brooke. [P.8] Of these Charles Brooke S.J., ordained at Maynooth, Ireland in 1802, came to live next door to the Mint residence of George Oliver. He died in 1852 and is said to be buried in St. Nicholas Chapel in the Mint. He was succeeded by a Fr. Thomas Lewis until October 1807 when the Reverend George Oliver arrived.

Meanwhile interesting developments were taking place in other Christian bodies. Dr. Alured Clarke was appointed Dean of Exeter Cathedral in 1741 and as an excellent example of Christian philanthropy was instrumental in the building of a new hospital for Exeter in Southernhay, opened in 1743 and made possible by generous public subscription. Black records that "in Exeter two Dissenter meeting houses were opened in about 1687 (and others in 1715 and 1760) followed by a Quaker meeting house in 1715, a Baptist Church in 1725, an independent chapel by 1744 and a synagogue in 1763." [11]

The Baptist Church is of particular interest to Sacred Heart parishioners since it is immediately adjacent to the South Street site. Arthur Gabb's History of South Street Baptist Church [P.11] summarises the main tenets of Baptist beliefs and of their complex relationships with other Christian groupings. This included having the dining hall of the Anglican Deanery purchased for their meeting place by Judge John

Carew in 1649. It was returned to the Deanery after the Restoration. Baptists have worshipped in premises in South Street since 1725. Their Church was fronted for many years by small cottages facing onto South Street. The church was rebuilt in 1822 and the old houses demolished in 1855; extant prints of these houses are good illustrations of the style of domestic buildings in South Street, and in Exeter city centre generally, in the years from 1600 to 1850. [30.3] Looking forward to the twentieth century, living older members of the congregation of the two South Street neighbouring churches report to me that there was in the years before 1945 some mutual suspicion and sense of mystery concerning religious worship in "the other place." It was perhaps the disastrous air raids during the Second World War which did much to bring Christian neighbours together, as both strived to save the adjacent premises from destruction by fire bombs. We return to that story in a later chapter.

Two other places of worship in South Street are near neighbours to the Sacred Heart Church - George's Meeting and Holy Trinity Church. One other Nonconformist chapel was close to the Catholic Mint chapel - the large Methodist Church at the Mint built in 1812. John Wesley had first preached in an Anglican City Church in 1739 but had been prevented from wider preaching engagements in churches. He therefore addressed large crowds out of doors, as did George Whitfield, a fellow evangelist. Eventually the Methodist Church between the Mint and Fore Street was erected in 1813 and re-built in 1970. [51.2] Methodists were attacked by hostile mobs in 1745 but survived and expanded in numbers, though they were fragmented into differing tendencies. "Methodism originated rather within the Church of England, which many of its zealots continue to see as their natural home, and not for decades did it clearly separate itself as a distinct denomination or connection." [51.2]

The two South Street chapels result from the expansion of Nonconformity in Exeter in the mid-eighteenth century. George's Meeting was erected in 1760 and named after George I. It is described by Pevsner as "by far the most interesting of the Nonconformist churches." It has been disused for religious worship since 1983 and has in 2005 been rebuilt as a public house. Holy Trinity (with its small central church turret) at the bottom of South Street has similarly been converted to use as a social club. Of the original churches in South Street in the nineteenth century only two survive.

Among the large number of new buildings in Exeter in the mid eighteenth century was a new bridge, opened in 1778, with a connecting new street going through the old city walls. Another was the Assembly Rooms built in 1769, now the Royal Clarence Hotel; and a third the General Bank opened in 1792, a neighbour to the other banks of the same period. The very modest Catholic Chapel in the Mint was in the centre of a neighbourhood which was experiencing much rebuilding, and modernising its amenities like pavements and street lamps. The mail coach in which George Oliver travelled down to Exeter was one of the new and speedier type operating between Exeter and London. Thomas Russel ran a service of horse-drawn wagons with its large head-quarters in South Street; it coped with increased long-distance goods traffic before the coming of the steam trains and after the comparatively tentative use of canals in and around Exeter. Nevertheless considerable effort was spent on improvements to canals, and the large warehouses on the Quay at the bottom of South Street are evidence of the importance of Exeter's water-borne traffic; the whole Quay area has now been rebuilt as an area of residences and small-scale commerce. [33.3]

In its obituary notice of the "Rev. Geo. Oliver" published in the Western Times on March 30th, 1861 [P.13] there is an account of his arrival in the Mint on October 27th 1807. He found "a poor and rough mission" awaiting him and he had great difficulty in rousing the elderly woman caretaker. He had to provide wood for heating, food and drink from his own pocket. Not only were the premises of the chapel and house extremely modest; the attitude to the Mission Chapel in the city generally seems to have been suspicious or even downright hostile. [P.19] However, the 1778 Relief Act had repealed the harsher provisions of the 1688 Act by which Catholics had been excluded from a large number of professions and public offices. Not all Catholic disabilities were removed by the 1778 Act but it gave new heart to a minority whose hopes for revival now grew. It off-set the depression at the death of Bishop Challoner in 1781.

Fig 9 Dr. George Oliver

Kennedy lists the disabilities still suffered by Catholics to which the Catholic Committee at national level drew the attention of Mr. William Pitt in 1788. [38] In the

Western District Bishop Walmsley had been appointed in 1770 [P.4] (Kennedy gives the date of appointment as 1764); he had his episcopal residence in Bath. The potential of anti-Catholic feeling was shown by the riots instigated by Lord George Gordon, both in London and in Bath. In the latter city the scholarly Benedictine Bishop Walmsley had his house attacked and his books and archives burnt. [38] There is no record of similar violence in Exeter.

As a concomitant to the 1778 Relief Act, Catholics were required to take an oath of loyalty to the sovereign - in this case to King George III. The Catholic Committee, consisting largely of laymen, found itself at variance with the Vicars Apostolic over the oath. The representative of the Western District on the Committee was Lord Clifford, and he seems to have adopted the general Committee attitude of merging as far as possible with the generality of English society, and of disproving any suspicion among the other Christian citizens that Catholics were influenced, still less led, by ecclesiastics identified with foreign countries or cultures. [38] The Committee also wanted the re-appointment of Catholic Bishops and the discontinuation of the "Vicars Apostolic" arrangement. It furthermore argued for the establishment of an English college in England to replace those in Belgium and France, thus giving greater national identity to English Catholics. Over most of these questions there is evidence of serious tension between the Vicars Apostolic and the Catholic Committee; this led to questioning of the mandate and representativeness of the Committee. [38] Charles Butler, as Committee Secretary, negotiated with the Prime Minister, William Pitt, over the extension of Catholic relief. Pitt logically enough maintained that similar relief would have to be granted to all Dissenters, of whom, in Devon for example, there were a substantial number. [38] The Committee also circulated the "Protestation" against false accusations of unpatriotic belief made by certain Protestants; it was signed by 1,500 of whom 240 where priests. [38] It was an episode in a long and complex (sometimes bitter) debate within the Catholic body which delayed until June 1791 the Royal assent to the Catholic Relief Act; even that Act left Catholics without full civil rights. [38, 51.2]

One minor factor in delaying the enactment of the 1791 legislation was the affair of the Prince of Wales and Mrs. Fitzherbert ; a person of good Catholic up-bringing , twice widowed and at the centre of a Richmond , Surrey social circle of renown. Of the Prince of Wales it was uncharitably said that his devotion to Mrs. Fitzherbert was the one redeeming feature in his character. They were married by a clergyman of the Church of England in December , 1785 . It was not clear how far familiarity with this cause célèbre penetrated to local Catholic groups or indeed to Anglican parishes, but it certainly stirred up lively controversy about the validity of the Prince's marriages to Mrs. Fitzherbert and to Princess Caroline. [38, 80]

The debate in the House of Lords over the Bill which in amended form became the 1791 Act had been enlivened by a remarkable speech in Parliament from Dr. Samuel Horsley, Anglican Bishop of St. Davids. He fully exposed the controversy within the Catholic body, but pleaded for modification to the Bill which would make it acceptable both to the Catholic Committee and to the Vicars apostolic. His intervention was effective enough to ensure that the 1791 Act entailed an oath similar to that involved in the First Emancipation Act and acceptable to Catholics in England. It was an unexpected example of Episcopal collaboration. [38]

The French Revolution of 1789 had resulted in the persecution of French clergy and of members of religious orders; particularly from Brittany, Normandy and Paris. The Revolutionary Civil Constitution of the Clergy did not appear at the time to imply the implacable conflict which ensued from it. [28] As was implicit in the Déclaration des Droits de l'Homme et du Citoyen, "The religious order was thus brought into line with the civil order, the edifice of the Church structured on that of the State …its links with the Papacy were severed; now it depended entirely on temporal government." [28] Hardly surprisingly the Civil Constitution of the Clergy was condemned by the Papacy in 1791; by the following year there was passed a decree on the deportation of refractory priests from France. One of the practical results of the French Revolution upon English civil life (as distinct from military conflict) was to receive an influx of religious refugees. In 1685 the Revocation of the Edict of Nantes had led to a wave of Huguenot refugees bringing with them special skills to London, Plymouth and elsewhere. The 1789 Revolution brought within a few years waves of French clergy who were received with a warmth surprising in the light of traditional suspicions between the two neighbouring countries. Influenced no doubt by Edmund Burkes' 1791 oration in the House of Commons, large numbers of English citizens - irrespective of their religious affiliation - organised help and relief for the French emigrés. Sir Samuel Romilly commented wrily on "The phenomenon that priests should be walking unmolested in London only 12 years after the Gordon Riots." [38] The Catholic Church in England clearly benefited from the influx of priests and religious who helped with the Catholic revival especially in education. The Revolution also entailed the dissolution of the English colleges and convents on the continent and obliged Catholics to train more from their own native resources - though with substantial help from neighbouring countries, especially Ireland, as we shall note later.

The outbreak of the wars with France in 1793 had a considerably adverse impact on the trade of a city like Exeter with a long-developed port. Instead the commercial life of the city altered its administration, and encouraged comparatively wealthy settlement (as well as very poor housing for unskilled workers) and small-scale skilled trades. Following the battle of Waterloo in 1815 there was a serious recession [33.3] which affected the price of agricultural produce and caused urban unrest. The demand for political reform grew and in troubled times economic growth was limited as in the case of Exeter in the 1820s. [33.3] Bishop Philpotts voted against the Reform Bill in the House of Lords which led to attacks upon the Bishop's Palace in Exeter. [33.3] George Oliver's early years at the Mint Chapel, and indeed the majority of his residence there (and down to the move to South Street) were a time of considerable economic change and political unrest. Following the French Revolution the Jesuits were forced to leave Liège and established their college at Stonyhurst; the Benedictines came to Ampleforth . George Oliver was educated at Stonyhurst, though he never joined the Jesuits. He was ten years old when the 1791

Act was passed and Catholic worship was legalised, though with certain conditions, as has been chronicled above. Ordained priest in 1806 he was appointed to the Exeter mission in the following year.

George Oliver must have started on his historical research shortly after his arrival at the Mint. The City Chamber resolved in 1817 to "form some plan for the arrangement of the Deeds and Records of this Body," and it entrusted the task to George Oliver. Four years later, in collaboration with Pitman Jones, a local attorney, he completed his examination of the Chamber's records. Jones was paid eighty guineas for his services in 1821 and two years afterwards Oliver received an engraved piece of plate of the same value. Oliver published his work on "Historic Collections relating to the Monasteries in Devon" in 1820 and dedicated it to Lord Clifford of Chudleigh. There followed his history of Exeter in 1821. Exeter City records include a letter of thanks for the gift from George Oliver. In a sympathetic, though critical, review of Oliver's History of Exeter published in 1961, W.G. Hoskins, himself the foremost Exeter historian, refers to it as "the first serious attempt at a history of Exeter." I have drawn upon it at many points in this brief history of Sacred Heart Parish and its predecessor Mint Chapel.

It will be clear from any examination of Oliver's work in the city of Exeter that he was widely accepted as a scholar of repute and a leading citizen. Whilst continuing as a devoted pastor in difficult surroundings he was concerned to establish Catholics in civic as well as in Christian life. The Catholic Emancipation Act of 1829 gave him great joy; he preached a fulsome and enthusiastic sermon on the next Sunday after the passing of the Act, proclaiming that "Every brand, every badge on inferiority, is removed from our very sight. We stand erect as freemen … Eternal gratitude be ours, to the House of Brunswick, and to our Patriot King … Towards our Protestant friends and advocates … we are bound to cherish the most affectionate and grateful attachment." [50.3] Certainly Catholic peers now took
their seats in the Lords and five Catholic M.P.s were elected at the 1830 General Election. [38]

George Oliver's civic and pastoral dedication was soon to be put to the test. In 1832 in the unhygienic surroundings of the poorer quarters (especially the Western Quarter not far from the Mint) an epidemic of cholera broke out and spread quickly. It lasted for some six months and 440 people died in Exeter city and suburbs. [33.3] George Oliver remained at his first post, ministering to the sick and dying throughout the epidemic. The unfortunate Bishop Phillpotts had left Exeter during the cholera, though he returned to lead a service of thanksgiving in the Cathedral at its end. George Oliver was thanked by means of a public subscription towards the cost of a silver salver engraved with an expression of gratitude, and with a pair of silver altar cruets. The latter are still kept at Sacred Heart Parish Church. Parish records show that the salver was on loan to the City Council in 1974 to be put on display in the Guildhall. [P.22]

As recorded in the Chapel Book [P.3], George Oliver went to the Guildhall to claim his right to vote in elections, since he was the occupant of the estate made over by Lord Clifford to the Catholic Minister when it was first set up at the Mint. He established his case and duly voted in December 1832.

During the wide national debate about Catholic Emancipation an influential pen was that of the Reverend Sydney Smith - " the ancient and amusing defender of our faith" (Daniel O'Connell), an Anglican clergyman and a great wit. Among his many writings between 1807 and 1843 was his advocacy of Irish clergy endowment and English Catholic Emancipation. Against the background of the wars with France and the threat of Napoleonic invasion Sydney Smith ridiculed the "No Popery" campaigns, arguing that it was in England's own interest to replace bigotry with toleration. Among the many targets of Sydney Smith's barbed witticisms was the then Bishop of Exeter, of whom Smith is reported to have commented: "I must believe in the Apostolic Succession, there being no other way of accounting for the descent of the Bishop of Exeter from Judas Iscariot." This acerbic comment referred to Henry Phillpotts, Bishop of Exeter from 1830 to 1869. Of him it has been written that "Roman Catholics and Nonconformists with their new legal freedom could be ignored provided they did not get too big for their boots." [33.3] It may well be that Bishop Phillpotts appears to have been a somewhat quarrelsome prelate, but he did preside over a diocese which showed impressive expansion during his episcopate. That included the foundation of St. Lukes College of Education (since 1978 part of Exeter University). Diocesan administration and liturgical practice were rationalised. Bishop Phillpotts was strongly opposed to Calvinism (as well as Catholicism). He refused to appoint a Calvinist minister to the living of Brampford Speke, a village outside Exeter. The minister appealed to the Privy Council and won his case. This of course raised the whole question of patronage in clerical appointments and gave rise to some turmoil. Bishop Phillpotts' chaplain, William Marshall, became a Catholic - as indeed had John Henry Newman before the 1850 events. Philpotts was also involved in a second public controversy over the wearing of surplices, which caused riots at St. Sidwell's Church in Exeter, where a member of the Courtenay family was priest. [51.2]

In assessing the "Victorian achievement" in the Church of England, Canon John Thurmer comments: "The 'ideal' Church model of the bishop ruling his diocese and the parish priest ministering to his parish operated more completely in the nineteenth century than ever before … It was the Victorians who made church buildings theatres of sacred music and liturgical drama, and because of this their own buildings, however lovingly Gothic, showed significant differences from the middle ages they claimed to revere." [51.2] One cannot fail to hear echoes of Thurmer's comments in discussions of the Sacred Heart Church building. There was public controversy within the Catholic body at the time between the architects Augustus Pugin and Ambrose Phillips and Cardinal Wiseman over Church architects, in particular about rood screens (even when the latter were symbolic rather than structural). However, between 1837 and 1845, thirty-five Catholic churches were built in the Neo-Gothic style, including St. Chad's Cathedral in Birmingham. Plymouth Cathedral was built in 1858.

The mid-nineteenth century has been accurately depicted as a time of Catholic Revival, after the long dark days of persecution. There was a minority reluctant to take up the challenge of open religious practice and active citizenship. Bishop James Bramston of the London District, for example, warned of its dangers and seemed to show a readiness to cling on to the devout traditions of an oppressed Catholic minority. [38] However, "normal" episcopal government was being restored to the Catholic Church in England, despite some shrill protests to the provocatively jubilant pastoral letter written by Cardinal Wisemen. [38] Opposition certainly continued, as did insistence that Catholic Bishops should not assume the titles of Anglican Sees. Guy Fawkes bonfires in 1850 included the burning of effigies of the Pope and the new Cardinal Archbishop of Westminster. Over 30,000 signatures had been obtained in Devon to a protest against the 1829 Emancipation Act, and Exeter City Chamber presented six petitions to government against conversions to Roman Catholics during the years from 1813 to the date of the Act itself.

There was almost equal outcry in Anglican circles against the revival of High Church practices, referred to in contemporary Exeter press reports as "Puseyism." [51.2] These can be linked with John Henry Newman's Tracts and his eventual conversion to Catholicism in 1845. Newman's "Idea of a University" made its mark intellectually, though his attempt to persist with the foundation of a Dublin Catholic University failed after three years. [80]

Meanwhile the immigration of French Catholics already noted was followed from 1846 by another immigration of a very different kind. The disastrous potato famine in Ireland brought starvation and enforced emigration to thousands of labourers and tenant farmers. [30.1] In the newly industrialised cities of the North and the Midlands - to a lesser extent the West of England - Irish workers found a living in docks, factories, and furnaces, and set up a pattern of later immigration in professions like nursing and medicine which persisted to the late twentieth century. Irish priests accompanied many of their countrymen and the English Catholics benefited from their continued ministry down to the present day. Two comparatively recent religious orders - the Passionists and the Rosminians - devoted much of their early pastoral care to recently arrived Irish migrants. This may have distracted them at first from sharing English evangelisation, though the Rosminians at any rate became notably active in English school education. The Irish migration might also have contributed to anti - Catholic prejudice against renewed Italian and Irish influence just at the time when Catholics were proving again their English bona fides. [80]

Statistics prepared and published by Bishop Peter Baines OSB in 1840 show 8 Catholic Missions in Devon, including the one in Exeter, and with a Devon County total of 3,368 Catholics served by 8 priests. There is some discrepancy between these figures and the results of the National Census of Religious Worship carried out in 1851. [17, 51.2]   The Census statistics show 8 Roman Catholic places of worship in Devon, including Exeter, with an attendance of 1,813. This compared with 549 Church of England places of worship with an attendance of 227,000. The Nonconformist share of all attendances was 54.9%. Roman Catholics in Exeter are shown as having just under 1% of all Devon attendances at religious worship. The East Stonehouse district of Plymouth is shown as having the highest Roman Catholic attendance in Devon - at 15.3% of all attendances there. There are a number of possible explanations for the discrepancies between the Baines and the National Census statistics; these include the definition of being a Catholic and being an "attender"; the methodology of the surveys on which the figures are based; and the frequency and nature of the services involved. Some of the same problems still bedevil the collection of reliable data in this field, even though methods of collection and classification are now far more sophisticated.

Fig 10   *Interior of St. Nicholas Chapel, The Mint - end of 19th Century*

We do not know the social composition of the small Catholic body of faithful Catholics who frequented the Mint Chapel. We know that Dr. George Oliver put the number of communicants at 28. [P.3] We know too quite a lot about the landed gentry whose contribution to keeping the Catholic faith alive has been appreciatively noted. [51.2] Hoskins describes the Exeter physical environment of the time as "old and dirty, still largely medieval in appearance with its narrow, overhung streets, with gutters (known as Kennels) down the middle to take away the rainwater and the lesser filth, and its multitude of dark lanes feebly lit by oil lamps" [33.3] Todd Gray has rescued from oblivion reports appearing in the local press in the 1850s of living conditions in the "West Quarter." [30.1, 30.2] Most of the tenements were later cleared by City Council authority or by Second World War bombing. The overcrowded conditions of the West Quarter were in sharp contrast to the fine villas being constructed in areas like Pennsylvania, Heavitree and St. Leonards. The journalist of 1850 in the local newspaper recounts his meeting with an Irish mat-maker working in his tenement. He and his neighbours retain "the ancient faith"; they have a Catholic Prayer Book, though no Bible and they praise the kindness of "Mr. Eccles" who frequently calls. Many other tenement dwellers survive by selling tape, matches and sundries. All are indignant at the recent rise in the price of bread which had prompted public disorder and sentences of imprisonment for those involved in 1854. [P.13] Many dwellers in the Quarter and in Frog Lane have lived there for between 18 and 50 years and have survived exposure to noisome stench, to rain and sewage effluence in many cases, but have refused assistance which would involve going into the Union house (Workhouse since 1835). The journalist reports favourably on the actions of "John Daw Esq. the excellent Chief Magistrate" who caused an investigation to be made into the sanitary state of Exeter. One result was the expulsion of some 400 pigs from various human abodes and their being driven across the bridge to St. Thomas.

It was in ministering to a "beloved flock" and in undertaking his historical studies that George Oliver spent 44 years in the small house in the Mint, in visits to historical sites and in the chapel of which happily we have extant engravings. In 1851 on Whit Sunday, Dr. George Oliver announced his retirement recalling that on his arrival in 1807 there were 28 communicants and now there were 180. Despite having installed a gallery in the chapel and putting extra benches in the centre, the accomodation was insufficient. George Oliver remained in the small house after his retirement, moving to a small room on the over-bridge between the house in the Mint and the former Priory. In 1844 Pope Gregory XIII had conferred on George Oliver the degree of Doctor of Divinity in recognition of his scholarly writings, his ecumenical work in Devon and his devotion to the chapel of St. Nicholas in the Mint.

He died in 1861 and is buried in that former Mint Chapel, as is commemorated on a plaque on the wall of the present Mint Building opposite St. Nicholas Priory. 21, The Mint remained in the hands of the Catholic parish and in Catholic Diocesan ownership. A small school was started at the Mint premises and remained operational till 1959, when it was transferred to Holloway Street and later to St. Nicholas School in Matford Lane. A caretaker remained on the Mint premises for many years, one of the last being Mrs. Bullen who was also in charge of school dinners at St. Nicholas School. After being let to the local authority for use by the Art and Design section of the College till 1991, 21 The Mint was eventually sold by the Diocese on a long lease of 125 years, with limitation on usage, to the Exeter Historic Buildings Trust. The Hall and Chapel were sold on a similar lease for conversion to residential accommodation.

Fig 11 *Mint Chapel Memorial Plaque*

21, The Mint owes its rescue and restoration to Councillor Carol Griffiths and her associates, including Lorna Till. It has been admirably restored with a large number of historical artefacts on display. The former refectory hall of St. Nicholas Priory is leased to adjacent St. Olave's Hotel. The Trust retains the large room under an arch-braced roof, and also the cloisters garden. Prince Charles visited the building in April 2004, and expressed admiration for the quality of restoration. It merits being visited by all Sacred Heart parishioners. One question remains to be resolved after all these years: where exactly is the burial place of Dr. George Oliver who laboured so long and so effectively in the Mint?

The Gazette commented at his death "It would be difficult to find among the citizens of Exeter one more generally esteemed by all the classes of the community." Does his burial place not merit precise identification and honour?

Dr. Oliver was succeeded by Fr. James Eccles S.J. The increase in numbers of Catholics in Exeter and elsewhere in Devon made it essential to find new premises, both for the church and for a presbytery. Fr. Eccles and his parishioners raised the money for a Catholic Primary School in 1855, carrying forward the work of his predecessor. After a further succession of short-term Jesuit priests the Mint Chapel was formally made over to the Diocese of Plymouth. It fell therefore to Fr. George Hobson to work with Catholic lay people to make possible a move to the new site in South Street in 1884.

The search for a site on which to build a larger church continued. Eventually it was decided to negotiate for the purchase of some ground, used as a wagonners' yard, with a house attached, in South Street, previously the site of the old Bear Inn. On the 27th May 1873 it was bought for £4,650. [P.8] The site has a frontage onto South Street of 90 ft. and a distance of 145 ft. eastwards towards the Chauntrey. [P.10]

Among the benefactors who contributed to the cost of the ground purchase and the erection of the new church were:

St. Augustines Priory, Newton Abbot	£1,200
Mr. Abel Rainbeaux of Torquay	£1,200
Countess English, Teignmouth	£350
Lady Duncan	£240
Colonel Graham	£150
Mgr. Boone of Bruges	£100

The tenants were given notice to leave by April 1881 so that the ground could be cleared for the new church building according to the plan of Charles Edwin Ware of Exeter and Leonard Stokes of London (joint architects).

On July 1881 a meeting of Exeter Catholics was held, presided over by Bishop W. Vaughan. A committee to collect subscriptions was formed with Mr. Mark Rowe as treasurer. They succeeded in raising £2,214 whilst the bishop collected nearly £7,200 from various sources. This was paid over to the builder in March 1885.

On April 19th 1882 ten tenders for the contract of the new church were opened by Rev. G. Hobson, Chas. E. Ware and Mark Rowe Esq. by commission of the Bishop of Plymouth. A tender of £9,066 was given by Mr. Henry Phillips of Exeter (later reduced to £8,878) and was selected. Work on pulling down the buildings and preparing the site started on June 6th. Signs of a religious house were found as the excavations were made for the church foundations. The Abbots of Tavistock had a town house here, as has already been mentioned. A 15th century window frame of stone was discovered and was incorporated into the stairway leading to the organ loft of the present church.

It was 28th March 1883 before the corner stone could be blessed and laid. The stone forms a portion of the base of the North Transept pier and was laid by Bishop Vaughan of Plymouth. The ceremony is said to have been viewed from the adjoining Canon's house by the Bishop of Exeter, who wanted to learn the orthodox manner of carrying a crozier, [P.8] but the story smacks of folk lore, and the original record of such an event is missing.

Originally it had been thought to build only the sanctuary, transepts and three bays of the nave, but as subscriptions came in beyond anticipation it was settled to complete five bays of the nave and aisles, and finally to add also the west narthex, and tower, with its entrance up to the belfry. (The original detailed plans are in the parish archives).

The tower bell, manufactured in the foundry of Mr. J. Murphy of Dublin, weighs over 19 cwts. and gives a clear mellow sound. Around the upper portion is a fillet in which, on one side, there appears the inscription:

JOANNES MURPHY, DUBLIN AD 1884

Below it there is the Irish harp inscribed with a wreath of shamrock. The inscription on the opposite side runs as follows:

IN HONOREM SANCTI BONIFACI EPISCOPI ET MARTYRIS

and below there is a representation of a watch tower with an Irish wolfhound lying at the base. The bell was given by Mr. John McAlister of Penzance and was blessed in the incomplete church by Bishop Vaughan, assisted by the Rev. Geo. Hobson and six other clergy, mainly Redemptorist Fathers from Teignmouth, on 18th July 1884. The bell was hung under an improvised covering in the tower, pending the erection of the belfry.

The presbytery was occupied by Fathers Hobson and Barry on November 13th 1884. On November 17th 1884 Father Hobson gave the ritual blessing to the complete edifice, and on the following day said the first Mass in it at St. Joseph's altar. The Bishop of the Diocese said the first Mass at the High Altar.

The Church of the Sacred Heart of Jesus was solemnly opened at 11:00 on November 18th 1884 in the presence of an Archbishop, three Bishops and about seventy clergy, nearly all from the Diocese of Plymouth. In the long procession from the Sacristy, the choir dress of secular clergy was intermingled with the habits of members of religious orders - Benedictines, Basilians, Dominicans, Canons Regular of the Lateran, Franciscans, Marists and Redemptorists; followed by the Bishop of Plymouth and the Chapter in their Canonicals. The new church was in a very unfinished state at the opening, for there were merely tables on the High Altar and St. Joseph's Altar and there was no altar at the Lady Chapel. Mr. Alfred Pursell subscribed £250 towards the High Altar. [P.12]

Catholic Church of Sacred Heart, Exeter.

Fig 12 *The church tower showing the temporary wooden cap*

The details of the church's construction already noted in Chapter 2 are as follows:

- The exterior of the church is 145 ft. long by 90 ft. wide.
- The walls are of blue limestone from quarries at Westleigh and Chudleigh, with Bath stone dressings.
- The roof was of Welsh slate and required replacement in 1984 and major repair in 2000.
- Inside the church the roof is of vaulted English oak, and the height from floor to this roof is 60 ft.
- The inside walls are of veined pink stone from Poccombe Quarries, with Bath stone dressings.
- The large columns supporting the Chancel Arch are of Corsham and Portland stone.
- The columns supporting the bays in the aisle are of brown Poccombe stone with Portland stone bases.
- The High Altar is of Beer stone, with scenes depicting the seven Sacraments sculptured on panels of Beer stone around it.
- On the Feast of Pentecost 1887, the ornamental reredos of Beer stone was completed right across the apse, and an alabaster and marble Tabernacle, designed by the Rev. Alexander Scoles of Bridgwater, was installed.

The Lady Altar was erected by public subscriptions and was inaugurated with High Mass on 2nd May 1887. The Tabernacle here is similar (but smaller) to the Tabernacle on the High Altar, being designed by the same artist. It is decorated with a sculpted scene of the marriage feast at Cana and another of the crucifixion. The Altar of St. Joseph was the gift of Mrs. Alexandra Knight of Axminster, in memory of her deceased husband, Joseph Alexander Knight - December 26th 1881 - *"for the repose of whose soul she begs the prayers of the faithful."*

Miss Middleton from London presented the Stations of the Cross painted on zinc in Munich with dark oak frames, and erected on 18th April 1886. On the Christmas following she also gave the wrought iron rood screen with originally seven Sanctuary lamps, the work of Hardman, Powell & Co. of Birmingham.

CHAPTER 6

From 1884 - 1918: A Parish Church

With excusable hyperbole the opening of Sacred Heart Church on November 19th 1884 was described in a local newspaper report thus: "There can be no question that from the time of Elizabeth downwards there has never been seen within the ever-faithful city such a gathering of mitred prelates and robed priests as will be witnessed on the 18th November." [(P.12)] It is interesting that the press report should find it appropriate to refer to the Exeter City motto "Semper Fidelis" (ever-faithful) on the occasion of the opening of a minority church towards which there had only recently been hostility in some local quarters. No doubt the unremitting labours of Dr. George Oliver at the Mint had contributed to a public attitude of greater tolerance and sympathy.

The press reports of the opening also contain details of the internal structure and furnishings. Among them was the pulpit. Originally both the local press and two contemporary photo-lithographs by Leonard Stokes, the architect, show a pulpit in the niche on the north chancel of the church. In 2004 that space is largely occupied by a statue of the Sacred Heart. The photo-lithographs in Todd Gray's admirable collection of "Exeter Engraved" [(30.4)] presumably show what was planned by the architect rather than necessarily what was built and used. The stone pulpit in the nave of the church is very little used now and the lectern for reading during mass is on the left-hand side of the chancel (as you stand facing the altar). There has been continuity in prayer and in announcing the gospel to parishioners, but change in the location of the pulpit from which the word of the Lord is promulgated.

There was mention in the press reports of the opening of the church of a wooden pulpit from the Mint Chapel being transferred to the new church. It is not clear when this was removed and the stone pulpit in the nave installed. There is no date on the stone pulpit and the parish archives do not give us one. The oldest parishioners whom I have interviewed all state that to their knowledge, and that of their predecessor parishioners to whom they had spoken, the stone pulpit has always been in the church from the date of its opening.

The press reports of the opening also state that in a cavity within the place of the first laid stone there was placed a sealed glass bottle with the following inscription written on vellum by Mr. F. Walker:

Anno Domini MDCCCLXXXIII Die 28 Martii
Lapidem Istum Primarium Hujus Ecclesiae
Sanctissime Cordi Domini Nostri Jesu Christi dedicatae
Posuit Reverendissimus Dnus Gulielmus Vaughan D.D.,
Episcopus II Plymuthensis Anno VI. Sanctissimi
Dni Nostri Leonis Papae XII; Victoriae in
Britaniis feliciter regnantis Anno XLVI.
Georgio Franciso Hobson Misso, Apco Missionem Curante;
Carole Edwin Ware et Leonardo Stokes Architectis.

A translation of the above inscription would be:

"On the 28th day of March in the year of Our Lord, 1883 the Most Reverend William Vaughan D.D. Second Lord Bishop of Plymouth laid the first stone of this church dedicated to the most Sacred Heart of Our Lord Jesus Christ; this was during the sixth year of the reign of our most Holy Father Pope Leo XII; in the forty sixth year of the happy reign of Victoria in Britain. George Francis Hobson being charged with the care of the Mission; Charles Edwin Ware and Leonard Stokes, the architects".

Present-day parishioners will be re-assured that Bishop Graham's account of the site states that it was chosen as "being easy of access to the respectable and nearer to the poor, containing also space for a large church, for schools and a priest's house, so it was felt desirable to secure it as a future site for such in place of the Mint" [29]. The schools were not built on the site, though one was before long established in Palace Gate around the corner. The presbytery was established in the large brick building whose style is in doubtful harmony with that of the church and one of whose former uses was that of a warehouse. However, it must have provided much better living quarters than those in the very modest Mission House at the Mint. [P.3]

Negotiations for the purchase of the site included some with the Charity Commissioners regarding the ownership of part of it by the Grendon Charity, a body founded in 1411 and the owner of a number of Exeter Almshouses. [P.3]

By 1895 Sacred Heart Church had been named by a Plymouth Diocesan Synod as a "Missionary Rectory" and during a mission given by a Capuchin priest 60 people were confirmed in the Catholic faith. Six years later Bishop Graham is reported to have confirmed another 67 people, and in July 1904 to have confirmed 58. [29]

The first High Mass for over 300 years was sung by the Diocesan Bishop on March 25th, 1906. Bishop Vaughan had successfully asked the Holy See for a co-adjutor bishop for Plymouth diocese, to which appointment Canon Charles Graham was consecrated in October 1891. [38, P.8]

The Advent Pastoral letters from 1865 to 1914 give illuminating commentaries on diocesan and parish events, including those at Sacred Heart Exeter. Copies are in the parish archives. The appointment of Canon Hobson (as he had now become) as the first Missionary Rector is announced in the Advent Pastoral of 1895. In 1897 there is a record of "The Sovereign's Diamond Jubilee Year." It was in that same year that the Sisters of the Presentation of Our Lady from St. Andéol purchased and occupied Palace Gate house and grounds very close to Sacred Heart church, thus establishing a close relationship which lasted over a hundred years. [P.8, P.9]

In the Advent Pastorals can also be found references to the settlement in the diocese of orders of French nuns (to a lesser extent Belgians) particularly in connection with ventures in school education. Among them was a religious order from Rennes in Brittany who settled in Swanage and Ilfracombe. It was with Rennes that Exeter City was to establish a flourishing twinning arrangement. Visitors from Rennes have been welcomed to Sacred Heart parish.

We need to remember too the continuing help by priests from Ireland over the period from 1884 to 1914 - and well beyond it. [32] An interesting example, to which Monsignor Harry Doyle has drawn my attention, was that of Patrick Augustine Sheehan who was to become a prolific author of popular novels in Ireland. After ordination at Maynooth, Fr. Sheehan found no vacancy in the (Irish) diocese of Cloyne and at the age of 23 was assigned in 1875 by Bishop Vaughan to a curacy at Exeter under the rectorship of Canon Hobson. Sheehan's nine months in Plymouth before being assigned to Sacred Heart Parish must have quickly hardened him to an unfamiliar, even hostile, environment. During his rectorship, in the year 1875, Canon Hobson is reported by Sheehan's biographer, Michael Barry, to have thought he might have a vocation to a religious order. [8] He went away from the Exeter Mission for about a year, leaving the young Irish priest in charge of the Mission. The experience clearly opened up new social horizons for him and on his return to Ireland he reported favourably on the Mission experience.

In 1909 Monsignor Hobson (as he now was) became seriously ill and was medically advised to retire from "all responsible ecclesiastical work." This included the post of Provost in the diocese. In a warm tribute to his fifty years of work in Plymouth diocese, including his forty in Exeter, the Advent Pastoral letter of 1909 reports his retirement at the Presbytery in South Street "with an extra assistant to carry on the duties under his regulation." He died two years later. [P.1] A tablet on the wall of the tower of Sacred Heart church is inscribed:

"In pious memory of the Right Reverend Provost Hobson for forty years Rector of this Mission 1871 - 1911, through whose unflagging energy, perseverance and self-sacrifice this church was built and opened AD 1884. Laus Deo Semper."

It should be added that the records show that Canon Hobson took a full part in the life of the city, being a member, and then chairman, of the Board of Guardians, whose duties included the care of the poor. [P.8, P.10]

There seems to be general agreement among Exeter's historians that the period from 1870 to 1914 was one of expansion in religious observance. There was new building in places of worship by Anglicans, Baptists, Congregationalists, Methodists and by independent Chapels. The rapid development in Catholic parish worship was paralleled by that in other "faith communities." [32, 33, 38, 49, 51.2]

Various improvements in the furnishings of the parish church are recorded in the parish archives at this time. The pews in the nave were replaced in 1912 by 600 solid oak chairs (costing 14/- each!) Many of the usual fund-raising devices are reported as having been used by parishioners to pay for this new seating. Some of the "new chairs" still bear metal name plate holders which were used to reserve places for which seat rents were payable. In 2005 there is seating for about 400 people.

The old gas lighting installed when the church was built was replaced with electric lighting in the following year. The parish is indebted to a Miss Matilda Sharp whose beneficence met the cost.

A third innovation was yet to come, namely the installation of a modern central heating system. In 1914 the church was heated by two large coke burning stoves. The sacristy was heated by a small coal fire, whose grate could be seen until the renovation of the sacristy was carried out in 2004. It was not until 1926 that the central heating was paid for by the parishioners and was installed with a coal fired boiler below the sacristy. The two old coke stoves were then removed.

Records of the church services during the period immediately before, and during, the Great War of 1914 - 1918 show three Masses each Sunday (in Latin, with sermon and notices in English) and full celebration of Holy Week and of Christmas. A note is made in "Mr. Mac's" accounts of singing at all services being led by "the choir boys," but their number and formation is not known. One Father C.W. Smith is mentioned frequently as organist and choirmaster and having "trained the choristers to a very high degree of perfection." [P.1]

An "Ad Clerum" from Bishop Charles Graham dated June 2nd 1909 grants leave for daily benediction of the Blessed Sacrament during the octave of Corpus Christi, and once within the octave for Exposition "from Mass to evening service." The Bishop also reminds priests of the requirement from the Holy Father that there should be instruction about the Blessed Sacrament for three days after Corpus Christi ending in Benediction "and a special English prayer." Pope Leo XIII's prayer of consecration to the Sacred Heart is to be recited on the 3rd Sunday after Pentecost. [P.1, P.10] On the Sunday after the Feast of St. Peter and Paul prayers for the consecration of England to St. Peter are to be offered. "Let this be done," adds

Bishop Graham, "with a procession and all solemnity." There follows a reminder of the obligation of all priests to make an annual retreat and to tell the Bishop exactly when that obligation was met. There is a reminder that all altar breads used by religious communities must either be made from home ground flour or ordered from the Trappist Fathers at Woodleigh.

The Ad Clerum also contains very clear guidance on the matter of Catholic schools and the obligation of clergy and parents in that regard. We return to that question in a later chapter. Finally the Ad Clerum contains a reminder of the need for parish clergy to draw the attention of the faithful to the box in the church labelled "Peter Pence" and "to exhort them to place a contribution into it each week between June 29th and August 1st." The priest is to describe in his address to parishioners "how dutiful, Catholic and necessary an act such is." [(P.10)]

What must strike the modern reader of such an Ad Clerum is the length and breadth of the religious services prescribed, the evident expectation that parishioners would support them all, and the dogmatically assertive tone of the prescriptions. Clearly most Exeter parishioners were expected to spend a good deal more time in church than is now the case. It was taken for granted that all would attend Sunday Mass (in Latin). It was also expected that they would participate in other prescribed prayers and practices too. [(P.1, P.10)]

At Michaelmas, 1918 there appeared a second and revised edition of Adrian Fortescue's "Ceremonies of the Roman Rite Described," [(26)] prefaced by a highly commendatory introduction by Francis, Cardinal Bourne. In this substantial volume of over 400 pages are described in minute detail the conduct of every ceremonial in the Roman calendar. The book contains also a plan of a parish church choir and sanctuary, listings of church furnishings and decorations, and the vestments to be worn by celebrant, deacon and sub-deacon at Mass. (The deacon here refers to an ordained priest playing a defined role at Mass, not to a deacon in the current sense of a distinct order of clergy). As far as can be seen from notes left by "Mr. Mac" as sacristan and master of ceremonies for many years at Sacred Heart Church, Fortescue's guidance was followed faithfully. [(P.1)]

It has to be remembered that fasting from midnight before Holy Communion was general and that confession at least monthly was widely practised. Queues at confessionals on Saturday were long, especially during the Easter Duty period.

Reports in the Devon and Exeter Gazette describe the service of consecration of the church in May 1913 - "an elaborate ritual performed by Bishop John Keily of Plymouth." [(P.14)] The Bishop knocked three times on the main church door reciting in Latin "Lift up your gates - and let the King of Glory enter." The altars were duly dedicated, including that of St. Boniface, previously described in Chapter 1. There were soloists for the performance of Gounod's Messe Solenelle by a boy's choir under the direction of Fr. C.W. Smith. The Bishop granted an indulgence to all present, reports the Gazette, and as he left the church "bestowed by waves of the hand a blessing on all the congregation." The Bishop and a cross-section of priests and lay congregation then repaired to the Rougemont Hotel where they lunched with the Mayor and Mayoress of the city. [P.10] Despite this favourable civic connection and the press reports of the church consecration, there is no mention in the Flying Post of May 3, 1913 of any services at Sacred Heart Church, despite the long list of Sunday services at 33 other city Churches on that day. [P.12]

The same newspaper contained a long account of Midnight Mass at Sacred Heart church in 1914. Admission was by ticket only, of which 450 were issued. The "crib," which it is explained, "illustrated the Nativity" was screened off until the procession reached it. Somewhat dramatically the press account goes on: "A silence which could almost be felt prevailed over the church, while the congregation awaited with reverent mien the hour of the Nativity. Precisely as the clock struck the mystic hour an imposing procession came from the presbytery." As at the consecration of the church, Gounod's Messe Solenelle was sung at the High Mass which followed, in which a Mr. Wills, who had recently won a Gold Medal at the Eisteddfod, excelled in the tenor part. "An excellent address was given by Monsignor Gandy, the parish priest." Monsignor Gandy was at one time a priest of the Church of England and had served as a curate at St. Sidwell's church. [P.12]

These press accounts are supplemented by the entries in a (rather tattered) "Choir Journal, 1913 - 19" found in the parish archives. The choir at the time is listed as having eight trebles, three contraltos, one tenor, and three basses, one whom was also the conductor (Mr. C. Harvey). Music prizes were competed for in 1913 and the winners are listed with first place going to a treble with a score of 97%. [P.6]

The choir sang a Missa Cantata every Sunday morning including an Offertory motet, and there was Vespers, Sermon and Benediction on Sunday evenings. There were also Processions of the Blessed Sacrament on Feast Days and the liturgical celebrations of Easter and Christmas reported above. Gregorian Plain Chant features prominently in the music listed for all Masses. Disappointingly the Choir Journal record ends on April 11th, 1919. The financial accounts of the choir in the back pages of the Journal show that the members of the choir were paid an allowance. Among the intriguing entries are those for 10d for a telegram and 6 ½ d for lozenges!
[P.6]

The material environment of the parish was changing rapidly in the period between the opening of the church and the end of the World War. [33.3] The railway had reached Exeter from Bristol and London, Paddington in May 1844 and was extended to Plymouth four years later. What is now the South-West line to Waterloo was opened in 1860. Branch lines, notably that from Exeter to Exmouth, soon followed. The first motor car came to Exeter in 1897 and by 1904 there were twelve private cars registered in the city, but by 1912 there were 225. [33.1] In the Flying Post of May 3, 1913 a resident of New North Road is reported as being fined 10 shillings plus costs for driving up Bridge Street and failing to stop for a policeman, when travelling at a dangerous speed. [P.12]

The records of Deanery meetings of the clergy show their pre-occupations and the methods of sharing in spiritual development (as required by the Bishop). [P.5] One of them also shows the effect of public transport upon meetings. The times and days of Deanery meetings were modified to take account of cheap fares by public transport. This must have affected clergy from the north of the Deanery in particular, since meetings were almost always held in Exeter. Within the city, first the horse trams, and soon after the electric trams (from 1905), revolutionised general mobility, links between the city centre and the new suburbs in particular. The new Bridge over the Exe was opened in 1905 amidst public festivities and the electric trams managed the severe slopes down Fore Street to the bridge or down St. David's Hill to the railway station. South Street's slope presented a greater challenge - to which the trams were not equal. Generally people were becoming less tied to the locality which they could reach on foot. That applied to their work, their shops and to their parish. [5, 30.5, 33.3]

The population of Exeter showed rapid growth from 47,185 in 1901 to 59,164 in 1911. [33.1] In part this was due simply to the incorporation of St. Thomas district, across the bridge, into Exeter City in 1902. The demands upon a basic service like drinking water became urgent. The old conduits from which poorer citizens collected water were by the turn of the century quite inadequate and most were being removed. The one in South Street was removed in 1834 when the street was widened. [45, 30.4] The underground passages, now a popular tourist attraction, were excavated and built to carry water, enabling the supply to the Cathedral to be shared with the general city supply, especially through the Great Conduit at Carfax, later replaced by that in South Street. [30.5]

Political and military events that had involved all Exeter citizens, including the parishioners of the new church in South Street, were: the Boer War and the part in it played by General Redvers Buller, the municipal elections of 1900 bringing change from traditional Conservative to Liberal, balanced by the return of a Conservative M.P., the continuation of small industries such as tanning, the extraordinary stability of prices by modern standards, and the growth of an industrial enterprise like Willey's engineering. [33.1, 33.3]

The opening of the church in South Street in 1884 came at a time of change not only within the Catholic parish but also in the social, political and economic life of Exeter. All the other changes were over-shadowed by the outbreak of the Great War in 1914. Hoskins comments "The Great War of 1914 - 18 burst upon a pleasant old cathedral city, but after the first shock life went on pretty much as before." However, Hoskins also writes that "Regiments marched away to the war with bands playing and mobs of small boys trying to lead the way with home-made flags" [33.3] and he adds that "Wounded soldiers in blue crept around the city streets: one saw them everywhere."

The assassination of Archduke Ferdinand in Sarajevo had been reported in the *Flying Post* in July 1914, but greater prominence had been given to the possibility of civil war in Ireland. [P.12] By November 1918 the toll of heavy casualties was being recorded both in official statistics and in peoples' homes. War memorials were being erected everywhere. They included the Exeter War Memorial in Northernhay Gardens, and the modest plaque in Sacred Heart Parish Church. Here at 11 o'clock on November 11th each year parishioners still pause in silent prayer before Mass in memory of those killed in that First World War. On July 1st, 1916 on the first day of the Battle of the Somme 19,000 men were killed or died of their wounds. The Times of September 28, 2004 carries a report of a new visitor centre built on the site of the battle, and its report reminds us that the July Day in 1916 was "the bloodiest day in British military history." We know that the plaque commemorating the war dead of the parish promises that we will remember them at Mass in perpetuity.

CHAPTER 7

<u>1919 - 1945: Peace and War</u>

When the end of the "Great War" came in 1918 the Christian churches held services of thanksgiving for delivery, and of prayer for the repose of the souls of those thousands killed during it. In the local Exeter newspaper, the Express and Echo, there is an account of a service in the Cathedral, conducted by the Bishop with the support of the President of the Council of Free Churches. [P.13] There were few parishes who did not have at least one parishioner among the war dead. On August 19th, 1919 the thirteenth Sunday after Pentecost the usual Sunday afternoon service of rosary, sermon and benediction at Sacred Heart Church had added to it a Te Deum in thanksgiving for the end of the war. In July of the same year the annual parish garden fete was dubbed the "Victory Garden Fete." [P.1]

In 1918 Fr. Thomas Barney arrived in Exeter from Newton Abbot. He was to remain at Sacred Heart Church for 28 years and was buried in 1947 in the churchyard of St. Thomas Catholic Church on Dunsford Hill. He introduced several innovations into the services at Sacred Heart Church, especially the street processions. He was largely responsible for initiating the construction of the new church of St. Thomas of Canterbury as a "chapel of ease" to the Sacred Heart Church in the city centre.

Nationally the "coupon election" of December 1918 did not produce a government under Lloyd George's leadership which was ready to take bold initiatives to meet the enormous social problems and continuing political conflicts resulting from the war. [33.2, 42] The newspapers of the day, both local and national, express sentiments of concern for ex-soldiers, especially those disabled, and organisations like the British Legion had active branches in most cities, including Exeter, which furnished practical help. Some communications to the local press demanded restitution from Germany; such sentiments seemed quite at variance with the appeals for reconciliation and reconstruction expressed by Pope Benedict XV during the War, and by his successor after it ended. [38]

Such world-shattering events as the 1916 Bolshevik Revolution in Russia and the political unrest in much of Europe in the nineteen-twenties and -thirties may not have penetrated to a city like Exeter to any significant extent, but even Exonians cannot have remained unconcerned with the changes in political attitudes and groupings, although they were more evident in urban and industrial centres like London and in the north of England. As Robert Newton puts it in his *Victorian Exeter*: the 1914 - 18 war had been "more than an adventure in foreign parts." [49] There was an increased air of questioning the old order; in the general election of 1923 Exeter had its first Labour candidate after years of evenly-matched struggle between Liberals and Conservatives. [33.1]

The years of recovery after 1919 were by today's standards very tough. An older Sacred Heart parishioner has commented on them by describing Fr. Barney as "a good man for hard times," adding that the inter-war years certainly were "hard times." Unemployment in the South-West of England was less than elsewhere in the Kingdom but it was high enough to fuel demands for social reform. (P.15) The reforms in Poor Law provisions and the new system of National Insurance responded to an early need for social protection, but its long-term effect upon the inhabitants of the West Quarter of Exeter was minimal. Catholic parishioners now had the same rights as any other citizens (except for exclusion from the monarchy). The Representation of the People Act 1918 removed franchise disabilities from paupers who now had potentially greater political clout than ever before, but whose economic strength remained feeble. Women were given the vote in 1918, but only those over 30 years old; it was not till 1929 that there was full feminine franchise. (30.1, 33.1, 49)

There was indeed a Catholic response to all these social, economic and political changes. At national level, for example, Cardinal Manning's powerful intervention in the 1889 Dock Strike and his evident influence on the writing of the Papal Social Evangelical *Rerum Novarum* showed a sympathetic directness which a few years earlier would have been unthinkable for a Catholic Cardinal in England. (38, 18, 79) It partly compensated for Wiseman's triumphalist statements on the restoration of the Catholic hierarchy, which had caused much resentment among Anglicans. (38, 79) We do not have contemporary evidence of the extent to which the first social encyclical "Rerum Novarum" (1891) was studied and acted upon in Catholic parishes in England. On the fortieth anniversary of that document, in 1931 a new encyclical appropriately entitled "Quadragesimo Anno" appeared from Rome. It provided a reference point for parish circles and study groups as well as for action by Catholic trades unionists and employers. Nationally the Catholic Social Guild took up the study of the social encyclicals. The first notes we have of a "C.S.G." group in Exeter appears in 1953 in the Exeter Catholic Magazine; the Exeter group also attended the national Guild conference and discussed issues of the "Christian Democrat," the journal of the Guild. (P.16)

In 1937 there followed the Encyclical Divini Redemptoris which proclaimed unequivocal condemnation of Communism and advised prudent caution over the growth of Socialism. In the Catholic press of the time, and in popular tracts on social and political topics, writers like Hilaire Belloc, G.K. Chesterton and Eric Gill adopted an independent political line, espousing causes like Distributism or showing some sympathy with the regimes in Franco Spain or Fascist Italy. These were plainly at variance with the attitudes of Trades Unions and the Labour Party with which most Catholics who expressed any political views tended to sympathise. However, whereas Cardinal Manning had sympathetically intervened in the 1898 Dock Strike, Cardinal Bourne condemned the 1926 General Strike. (38, 79, 18)

During the 1914-18 war, Sacred Heart parishioners had given shelter and support to a number of Belgian refugees, some in their own homes and to others who were in camps near Honiton. [P.1] This was a closer example of solidarity with those in need than was the estimable and long-standing contribution of financial and spiritual aid in the parish through the red collecting boxes of the Association for the Propagation of the Faith and prayers for "the missions."

There had been a connection between Exeter and Brugge in Flanders, especially through the English convent there. Monsignor Boone of Brugge had given a generous donation to the funds collected in 1873 towards the building of Sacred Heart church. When the Belgian refugees returned home after the war ended in 1918 they donated, as a mark of appreciation, a banner of Our Lady to the Sodality of the Children of Mary in Sacred Heart Parish. [P.1, P.8]

Throughout the inter-war years there is evidence of much local activity of a charitable kind, for example through the parish branch of the Saint Vincent de Paul Society. (In a changed form the Society is still active today.) Parishioners also became more active in public life - in local government, in health concerns, in education and in support of family life. Until 1929 the administration of the Poor Law was in the hands of successor bodies to the parishes of the Established Church of England, but there is also good evidence of Catholic participation in them. [51.2]

Fig 12 *Blessed Sacrament procession, Palace Gate - early 1920s (?)*

The year 1929 saw the celebration of the centenary of Catholic Emancipation in all Catholic churches, including Sacred Heart, Exeter. [32, 38] In that same year "Mr. Mac" started his training for altar servers who are recorded as serving their first

Mass at St. Joseph's altar on the Feast of St. George, April 23rd 1929. [(P.1)]
Throughout the 1930s the Good Friday procession was organised from Sacred Heart
Church. At this and other processions altar servers carried a processional crucifix,
four bearers dressed in green robes shouldered a portable stand bearing a statue of
Our Lord carrying his cross; there were fourteen banners depicting each of the
Stations of the Cross set up around the city centre. The procession was formed by
the bearers and by a large group of the Palace Gate nuns, the boarders from their
school, the children from St. Nicholas School, and many parishioners. The route
followed was from the church in South Street, to the top of the street, thence to the
Guildhall in High Street, via Bedford Circus (now destroyed) to the G.P.O. in
Eastgate, down Southernhay to the Hospital, via Magdalen St. back to Sacred Heart
Church. Here a decade of the Rosary was recited for the repose of all who had died
since the previous Good Friday. Contemporary press photographs show very well
supported processions, apparently viewed with respect - and some curiosity - by
onlookers. [(P.1)]

There are in the parish archives two "Catholic Blotter Calendars and Yearbooks"
dating from 1928 and 1933. They are inscribed with the compliments of the clergy
and were presumably free to parishioners, the cost being met by the wide range of
advertisers supporting the issues. Apart from a generous supply of blotting paper,
the contents are a random mixture of local tradesmen's advertisements and of
devotional articles on, for example, the English Martyrs Blessed Thomas More and
Blessed John Fisher, a dramatic photograph of Fr. Barney and a more subdued
picture of one of his curates. The 1928 edition also contains a reminder of the
marriage laws of the church and a thought-provoking article on "The Church and
Science" by the Reverend Dr. John McQuillan.

The services in the Sacred Heart were:

Sunday Mass at 8 and 10:30
Compline, Sermon & Benediction at 6:30
Holydays of Obligation: Mass at 7, 8 and 10:30
Weekdays: Mass at 7:15 and 8
Wednesdays and Fridays: Benediction at 7:30

Services at other churches served from Sacred Heart were:

Bowden Hill, Crediton: Sunday Mass at 11:00, evening service at 7
33, The Strand, Topsham: Sunday Mass at 08:30
(Journeys from Exeter to Crediton for Boniface pilgrimages were
frequent; the current bus fare being 8d return!) [(P.1)]

Two commercial advertisements catch the eye in the 1933 Blotter:
The Cathedral Hotel at 194, High Street claims
"Catholics specially catered for - open Sundays."

Among the businesses in South Street at number 22, the
umbrella manufacturer, also selling "gold and silver mounted
walking sticks in great variety"

The year 1933 marked the nineteenth centenary of the Crucifixion of Our Lord
Jesus Christ. It was declared a "Holy Year of Jubilee" by the Pope. [38] The meaning
of this declaration was the subject of much commentary in the national Catholic
press as read by our parishioners; it was also the subject of an article in the 1933
Sacred Heart Directory, Calendar and Blotter. The "Directory" had now been
elevated to Diocesan status and was printed and published by Sydney Lee, The
Catholic Records Press, Haven Road, Exeter.

In 1932 two events of note had taken place, one ephemeral but commemorated, the
other of lasting significance to this day. On August 25th, 1932 the current Buckfast
Abbey information booklet records that the Abbey Church was consecrated by
Bishop John Barrett, in the presence of Cardinal Bourne, on the site of the medieval
Cistercian Abbey. [51.2] The Cardinal came up by car from St. David's station to
Sacred Heart Church on his way down to Buckfast. His visit allowed the priests and
congregation to greet him with a loyal address and to mark the occasion by erecting a
memorial tablet in the church porch. Very many parishioners from Sacred Heart
have followed the Cardinal's good example by making pilgrimages or tourist visits to
Buckfast Abbey.

By 1932 Exeter had two major Roman Catholic churches. On May 28th that year
within the octave of Corpus Christi the new church of the Blessed Sacrament was
blessed and opened in the Heavitree district of the city. [P.8] The programme for the
occasion (preserved in the parish archives) records that in a service set to last "about
half an hour" the Blessing would be carried out by Bishop John Barrett of Plymouth.
Application for tickets of admission had to be made to the parish priest for the next
day's Solemn Pontifical High Mass celebrated by the Bishop "assisted by priests,
deacon, sub-deacons, the M.C. and eight altar boys." The sermon was preached by
Dr. Ford. There followed an outdoor procession of the Blessed Sacrament and
Solemn Benediction.

The Blessed Sacrament Church is of a completely different design to its counter-
part across the city, being of Italianate style with a lavish use of marble and a
prominent feature of a large baldacchino. The church seats about 260. The
congregations of both parishes have grown closer together over the years especially
in support of St. Nicholas School, which serves all of Exeter or in social events in the
new Cardinal Newman Centre used by all Exeter parishioners, though established
through Sacred Heart Parish in agreement with the Diocesan authority.

In commentaries on the fabric of Sacred Heart church, several allusions have been
made to the bell tower. Parish records show that as long ago as 1919 it had been
agreed at a parish general meeting that a tower worthy of the church should be
completed and that the temporary wooden cover was unsatisfactory. [P.1, P.10] A letter

from the bishop favoured the completion of a stone tower. At another parish meeting an "executive committee" was elected to see the work through. The original architects, Leonard Stokes and Charles Ware, submitted a design, and a sketch of the proposed tower was exhibited at the church entrance. A wide range of fund-raising activities were promoted, and a substantial sum was deposited in the "Union of London and Smiths Bank." There then appears to have been a gap in the building programme and the next mention in the records comes in 1924. Several other demands upon parishioners were now evident and the parish priest made clear that a final decision must now be made and the tower completed. [29] Happily a proposal which emerged at one point to erect an illuminated cross atop the tower was abandoned. The tower, built in limestone with Bath stone dressings was put in place. It was to give the parish some repair problems, due to leakage, some years later.

In the parish archives is the minute book of some meetings of the Exeter Deanery Conference of Catholic Clergy. Apart from one meeting in Axminster all the meetings recorded between June 1918 and May 1950 were held in Exeter, most of them in Sacred Heart Presbytery. All clergy from all parishes in the Deanery were reminded by Ad Clerum letters from the Bishop of their obligation to attend the conferences which were regarded as opportunities for further in-service formation. At each conference an exponent presents a prepared case on a subject set by the Bishop, the other participants commenting and contributing to a solution. Between 1918 and 1950 subjects covered included: solutions to pastoral problems faced in parish work; the administration of the sacraments; pious devotions; Catholic schools; parish financial management; the administration and validation of marriages. Unanimity is reached in almost all cases, though some differences of opinion are recorded in the President's summing up.

Meetings were held at roughly quarterly intervals, though with some breaks. The minutes of the Conference in June 1918 record "Owing to the fact of his being at the Front - as chaplain to the Forces - Fr. Hayes, the late secretary, failed to supply the minutes of the last meeting." In 1940 the minutes of the June meeting record "Fr. Lombardi was absent, serving - we understand - in the army as chaplain." The minutes for that meeting were not in fact signed until June 1946 when conferences were resumed, at Palace Gate Convent.

The Conference minute book for 1924 records agreement that "Wednesday should be the day of the Conference as excursion tickets were issued from North Devon towns on that day of the week." There is a recurrent note of those attending having paid to the bishop the "cathedraticum," being a symbolic contribution by clergy to their bishop - a practice now discontinued. The Deanery conferences continue, though in somewhat modified form, the use of Latin being under review in 1940 and having been replaced by the vernacular today. The size and shape of the Exeter Deanery may be justified for clergy meetings or diocesan administration, but its relevance to the life of parishioners locally or at diocesan level deserves critical review.

Fig 14 *Parish procession at the Guildhall with Fr. Frank Balment, 1938*
[Arthur Brinicombe]

The policy of building churches in areas of new settlement, such as the Council housing estates of the 1930s, 40s and 50s may now be out-dated and to involve later painful decisions about the use of church buildings whose cost can no longer be justified. [54] Such is the case of St. Thomas of Canterbury, Dunsford Hill to whose fate we return in a later chapter. The church was built in 1938 in an area of new settlement which linked up the St. Thomas district across the bridge with Exeter city. The nearby suburb of Exwick has seen further intensive housing estates from the end of World War II down to 2004. Other factors, however, have entered the calculations of the numbers of Catholic parishioners likely to use St. Thomas Catholic Church for worship. A similar problem had to be faced later with St. Bernadette's Church in Whipton (now demolished). Fr. Thomas Barney died in 1947 and is - by special dispensation - buried in the garden of the church on whose building he had laboured so much. He had left behind him in Sacred Heart Church the large statue of Christ the King which he bought from Clery's showrooms in Dublin when he went to the Eucharistic Congress there in 1932. [P.1]

Once again, in 1939, the "normal" world of Exeter's city centre Catholic church dissolved into a war, the outcome of which cannot have been imagined in the parish. [33.1] After the "Phoney War" of the first year came the bombings, the battles, the Dunkirk trauma, the arrival of the American G. I.s in town, D-Day and eventual military victory. By the end in 1945 material life seemed to have an exhausted air about it [51.2] The spiritual continuity represented by the parish church was a reassurance. The return of Fr. Frank Balment from chaplaincy service in both Iceland and Burma showed continuity. Though Fr. Barney died shortly after the war, Canon Tobin's appointment and his twenty years as the post-war parish priest re-inforced a parish conviction that all would be rebuilt.

Mr. Lawrence McWilliam recalls the air raid precautions taken from the outbreak of the war in September 1939: "A large quantity of sand-bags were stacked high against the lower doorway of the porch … A very long wooden ladder was placed just inside the main door and reached to the top of the large west window … Buckets, long-handled shovels, stirrup pumps, steel helmets and gas masks all formed part of the equipment to deal with incendiary bombs." [P.1] This equipment was to be put to the test in the severe air raids on Exeter in April and May 1942.

The air raids on Exeter are described by Todd Gray in his meticulously documented study of "Exeter in the 1940s." [30.6] The Luftwaffe attacked the city on the nights of April 23rd to 25th, 1942. In those the police reported that 118 people were killed. [30.6] A high explosive bomb fell in the Cathedral Close, destroying the choristers school, several of the Canons' houses, and the Hall of the Vicars Choral, a short distance up South Street from Sacred Heart Church. [24]

It was the severe air raid of Monday, May 4th that caused most damage and which has gone down in the history of Exeter as its "Blitz." It was one of many raids on British cities in reprisal for the air raid on the ancient German city of Lubeck. Hoskins early general description of the Exeter raid was "Under a full moon about thirty German aircraft flew up the shining estuary about midnight, and for an hour and a half rained fire-bombs down upon the old city." [33.3] Evidence later assembled by Todd Gray from a contemporary National Fire Service report records that approximately 7,000 incendiary bombs and 150 high explosive bombs were dropped during this raid. [30.6] A vivid personal account of the fires across the centre of Exeter, including South Street, is given by James Whiteside, then the city's information officer, quoted by Gray. [30.6] Despite the enormous damage, almost miraculously casualties were comparatively low; "Altogether 80 people were killed, and rather more than a hundred injured" is Hoskins' estimate. Six churches were destroyed or severely damaged and the Cathedral itself suffered severe damage on the south side. [24, 33.3] James Whiteside's report contains a striking sentence "Everyone seemed to be dealing adequately with his own incendiary bombs." More detailed contemporary evidence illustrates how the bombs were dealt with at Sacred Heart Church and at Palace Gate Convent, around the corner.

There are several accounts of the events, with varying emphases on the part played by individuals. Sacred Heart Church escaped with comparatively minor damage, as did its immediate neighbour, South Street Baptist Church, even though most of South Street was engulfed in flames. Laurence McWilliam's notes of the event record that Fr. Thomas Barney showed tremendous courage in passing up buckets of water and of sand to his two curates Fr. Michael Walsh and Fr. P. Pedrick who were stationed on the flat roof of the presbytery. McWilliam quotes Don Busleton, the air raid warden for South Street, as having besought Fr. Barney to leave the building but the parish priest refused. [P.1]

Todd Gray reproduces a letter from Fr. Phil Pedrick to a correspondent, written only three days after the "Blitz." In it Fr. Pedrick endorses the descriptions so far quoted here, adding "all South Street is burnt down but for our church and house and the Baptists next door." [30.6] Referring to the Sisters in Palace Gate, Fr. Pedrick's letter recounts "Palace Gate has fire licking their wall but it stopped there. First they ran to get all our books down from our rooms & then they had to go over to see to their own home… We have had some meals at Palace Gate to relieve Miss Jane [the housekeeper], so much dirt and want of gas is a bother, but we have electric and a fuel stove. Fr. Barney stood up to the ordeal very well." [30.6] Canon Michael Walsh (who died in 2005) endorsed as an eye-witness the version of events recorded in Fr. Pedrick's letter.

Evidence from a worshipper at the Baptist Church next door is that two members of their church, Rev. Matthew Flint and Mrs. Flint, joined in efforts to save the two adjacent buildings, concluding that common efforts on that night may well have contributed to good relations between the two churches. [P.11]

The annals of Palace Gate Convent contain a vivid account of their involvement in the events of May 4th until the fires were brought under control at 6:50 in the morning of the next day.

"We looked outside. Fires were raging on all sides. The wind was strong and sparks flying over our heads spread the fires with frightening speed. The church and presbytery were in great danger. The priests carried on the struggle with splendid courage. Some of the sisters went to help them by passing buckets of water. The church was saved but the fire came closer to us. The cottage caught fire and then "Mitchell" wing. We decided to evacuate our children…They were taken to the reception centre in Roberts Road, where people were very kind to them…At five o'clock in the morning the priest gave us Holy Communion… On May 4th our day was spent in giving tea and food to the firemen…Our school had to be closed for a week. Several pupils did not return and the evacuees went back to London. May God be praised!" [P.9]

The evidence of those actually involved, or able to reproduce written evidence from them, is to be compared with an imaginative letter written to the editor of the Express and Echo shortly after the Blitz:

Angel of the Exe

Since your last issue I have been looking for a booklet about The Angel of the Exe my landlady, Mrs. Bastick, gave me. She was a Catholic but I cannot find it.

It was the night of our blitz, May 4. Exeter was burning - even the Lower Market, Sun Street. People were saving as much of their furniture as they could.

The Priest was on the roof of the Catholic Church, South Street, throwing incendiary bombs off. He looked towards the sky and saw the sign of the cross.

The wind changed and the people who were in the theatre in Mermaid Yard were saved.

A. J. Wippell, 16, Elaine Close, Beacon Heath, Exeter.

Fig 15 *Polish airmen present their flag to the city, 1942*
[Express & Echo]

Sister Edward Mary Milsom was at the Palace Gate on the night in question, having arrived in Exeter in July 1938. She supports fully the account given in the Annales but does not recall the sign of the cross in the sky. She does, however, remember Mrs. Bastick (mentioned in the letter) as "a dear elderly lady" who let out houses near to the Clock Tower and who lived for some time in a house in the warren of small streets at the bottom of Southernhay, near where the Southgate Hotel stands in 2005.

After the raids Hoskins recalls "I saw a gypsy tether his horse beside the ruins of South Street to feed on the grass-grown debris, and I saw an old lady picking flowers among the ruins." [33.1]

Nikolaus Pevsner sums up: "The German bombers found Exeter primarily a medieval city; they left it primarily a Georgian and Early Victorian city." Sacred Heart Church was (and is) part of that survival. Its post-war environment changed considerably, but its purpose and mission remained.

CHAPTER 8

1946 - 1984: Reconstruction and Renewal

The destruction from war-time bombing had been manifestly less in Exeter than in larger cities like London, Liverpool and Coventry, or in a nearer neighbour, Plymouth. Nevertheless it had struck at the very heart of the city; the cathedral had been seriously damaged, [30.3, 37, 75.1] and many other city churches destroyed. Sacred Heart Church had a remarkable escape, thanks to the valiant efforts of priests, parishioners and neighbours. As photographs and sketches show, it now stood amidst desolation in South Street. [30.3, 75.1] After dancing the conga on the bomb sites on VE Day it was time to pause, pray and take stock. [30.6]

Fig 16   *Procession up South Street - post-war ruins, 1945*
(In front: Laurence McWilliam; Left: Fr. Barney)

The experience of children's evacuation had impinged on Exonians in a different way from its effect on millions of British children. Exeter received many evacuees, some of whom were accommodated in St. Nicholas School in the Mint. Some teachers who came with the refugee schools lent their help to the parish church.

At the end of the war many Exeter children wandered over the ruins of the city centre, as one of them now recalls in his memoirs. It was a dangerous and dirty environment on the blitzed buildings at the top of South Street and in Market Street. [13, 33.1]

All parishioners of Sacred Heart, South Street had shared in the traumatic experiences of war-time. Reflecting on the war-time Beveridge Report and its aftermath I have summed them up as: "All citizens were likely before the war ended to have been subject to conscription into the armed forces, or to have moved away from home on essential war work, or to have been sent to coal mining as a Bevin Boy, or to have volunteered for a variety of new work experiences. Many people were now pre-conditioned to change in their lives after the war to an extent unthinkable before it". [41.4] Throughout the war services in Sacred Heart Church had to respect black-out regulations and to provide sand-bag precautions. Evening services had to be re-timed to avoid being held after dusk.

The end of the war ushered in a decade of reconstruction but in an atmosphere of comparatively drab exhaustion with continued rationing of food, clothing and other essential commodities. [33.1, 75.2] Parishioners who lived through the period have recounted personal experiences of that post-war environment; the names of those consulted are among the list given in the author's preface. Their accounts are similar to those given by a larger group of Exeter citizens interviewed for a survey conducted by the City Council under the title "Exeter Blitz", and published in 1987.

It could be argued that these experiences, coupled with likely personal and family traumas, would have pre-disposed parishioners to accept a new way of life in which the dramatic change of government at the 1945 General Election was matched by new forms of worship and of parochial association. [38] There is little evidence of that. The photographs of the parish procession striding up South Street in 1946 against a background of rubble and devastation could equally well be interpreted as an assertion of continuity of Faith and of its renewed public declaration. The Good Friday Way of the Cross had in fact to be discontinued from 1948 due to the danger from increased traffic. Inside the church a parish procession took its place. (Many years later a Good Friday procession promoted by Christians Together in Central Exeter was to take up again the outdoor Good Friday Walk of Witness and parishioners from Sacred Heart were to take part in it.) The immediate post-war years were marked by a reprise of Catholic activity, unavoidably modified during the war. [P.1, P.5, P.9, P.13]

On the other hand, some obligatory Catholic practices were relaxed. A communication from the Hierarchy in 1967 made it no longer a requirement to abstain from meat on a Friday, and the obligatory Fast Days were reduced to two. This announcement was accompanied by an exhortation to voluntary penance. It is not possible to measure the impact this had upon parishioners. One of the public and distinctive characteristics of Catholics had been the Friday abstinence from meat. "It is questioned whether it is advisable in our mixed society for a Catholic to appear singular in this matter", wrote the Bishops. [23.3] Eamon Duffy, however, points out "There is a world of difference between a private devotional gesture, the action of the specially pious, and the prophetic witness of the whole community, the matter-of-fact witness, repeated week by week, that to be Christian is to stand by the needy". [23.3] It could be argued that the specific outward signs of Catholic identity in an increasingly secular and commercial world were being diluted. Of course a belief in fasting, abstinence and almsgiving is something shared by Sacred Heart parishioners with many fellow Christians, though the specifics differ. [4, 51.2] (It is also of course an aspect of Muslim identity in a multi-cultural society.) [18]

"To observe the prescribed days of fasting and abstinence" is listed in the Catechism as the fifth of the five precepts of the Church, but their precise prescriptions are not given therein. [36] The obligation of Sunday Mass and of Holy Days of Obligation remains, though some variation in the list of the latter has occurred. [36] Sunday is seen in the Catechism as a successor to the Jewish Sabbath, transformed by Christ's enjoinder to commemorate the Last Supper by participating in the Eucharist.

Despite the increased mobility already noted from post-war days and the clear drop in Mass attendance over the years from 1960 onwards, [19, 23.3] the parish church remains the focal point for the essential weekly commemorative act of worship. The large national rallies such as those for the Sword of the Spirit during the war (August 1940), the Wembly Congress in 1950 and the later 1980 Liverpool Congress did not seem to reduce the significance of the parish; rather was it seen as the essential building block for such national affirmations of solidarity in faith. [41.2]

Parallel with this development was the increasing use of the concept of the "lay apostolate", a phrase notably popularised by Cardinal Bernard Griffin in a widely distributed Lenten Pastoral in 1952, the year of the World Congress on the Lay Apostolate in Rome. Certainly lay associations flourished in Sacred Heart parish in the nineteen fifties: the St. Vincent de Paul Society; a branch of the Catholic Social Guild; the Newman Association, for long organised by Hilda Swinburne and supported by Benedictines from Buckfast Abbey; the Catenians with their social and charitable witness. [P.1, P.14] All these activities survived the arctic conditions of the winter of 1947 and the rigours of the "fuel crisis". The Summer School of the Newman Association was held in Exeter in 1946.

Fig 17 *Hierarchy Centenary 1850 - 1950*
Pontifical High Mass, Sacred Heart Church, Nov 1950
(Left to Right: Canon P.J. Tobin, Bishop F.J. Grimshaw,
Archbishop Masterman, Bishop Murphy, Fr. W. Carter)
[Express & Echo]

In 1950 those active in Catholic associations joined in celebration for the centenary of the restoration of the Roman Catholic Hierarchy, a step still causing resentment (certainly at the time) among other Christians. [4, 38] The Mass of thanksgiving was celebrated in Sacred Heart Church by the Bishop supported by an enlarged choir (in the nave) and a large body of university staff and students. A photograph of the occasion shows the Bishop about to deliver his episcopal address from the pulpit in the nave.

Fig 18 *Pontifical High Mass, 1950. Bishop Grimshaw*
(note pulpit sounding board)

In the previous year the Sacred Heart parishioners had assembled with those from other Devon parishes, reinforced by visiting clergy, at Winslade School to commemorate the Western Prayer Book Rising of 1549. [P.1, P.9] The day's celebrations included a Grand Rally at the Exeter Civic Hall at which Bishop Grimshaw had spoken, followed by a talk from Sir Henry Slessor P.C. on "The Catholic Church and the State". G.T. Newman OBE rounded off the Rally with an address on "The Lay Apostolate". In an evident desire to emphasise the indigenous continuity of Catholic practice and Civic identity, the Rally ended with the singing of "Faith of Our Fathers" and "God Save the King". [P.1, P.15]

Fig 19 *Commemoration of the anniversary of the Western Rising, 1949 (From left: Monsignor Tobin, Bishop Grimshaw, Monsignor Ronald Knox, Abbot B. Fehrenbach OSB)*

During the immediately post-war years many improvements were made to the fabric of the church and presbytery buildings. A flight of stone steps was constructed from the South Street entrance to the presbytery, making the entrance door level with the hall and kitchen. This eliminated the troublesome exertion of clergy and housekeeper up 20 stairs to the front door each time the doorbell rang - as it very often does at the presbytery. Modernisation was carried out in the presbytery kitchen and bathroom. Repairs were made to the leaking church roof, and to the chancel arch. [P.1]

"Mr. Mac"'s note-book provides a systematic record of the repairs, renovations and decorations made from 1962 to 1982. The priest's sacristy and the altar servers (outer) sacristy were cleaned and re-plastered, old lino was replaced, windows were repaired, and enthusiastic work parties engaged in carpentry and even small-scale plumbing. The interior of the church and the statues in it, as well as the organ pipes, were given a thorough clean almost annually. A working party of some fifteen of us also tackled two major maintenance and renovation tasks: cleaning the interior roof and pillars of the church, and transforming the unused cellar at the lower level of the presbytery into a small but useful meeting room with an office and toilet. Robin Phillips is among those who played a consistent role in all the work of repair and decoration. The post-war programme just mentioned had of course to be repeated after 1984.

On one day each week from post-war days down to the present a dedicated band of church cleaners ensures that a high standard of cleanliness and polish is maintained. The Exeter Catholic Magazine for Spring 1956 contains a splendid piece of celebratory doggerel of which two verses are:

> Who makes the churches clean and neat
> And keeps the sanctuaries sweet
> Till folks say 'Don't it look a treat!'
>   - Us Marthas!

> Then, when St. Michael comes in state
> To open wide the Golden Gate -
> Who'll get there first as sure as fate?
>   - Us Marthas!

Linked to these efforts to make a place of worship as beautiful as parishioners can, is the work of the team of flower arrangers, for whose high standards at Sacred Heart Church tribute has so often been paid. So many parishioners have been involved that to single out any one risks invidiousness, but it is right to recall the leadership of Richard Dennis in routine flower arranging and in organising memorable flower festivals, and the quiet and self-effacing labours of the late Harold Moore, in the period under review and later.

In August 1948 altar servers from Exeter, accompanied by local clergy, attended a diocesan rally at Buckfast Abbey. The National Director of the Guild of St. Stephan, fully supported by Bishop Grimshaw, advocated the establishment of branches of the Guild wherever possible. "Mr. Mac", already experienced as an altar server himself, set about forming the Guild in Sacred Heart parish and by the end of the same year had enrolled eight members. By 1966 three servers had qualified for the award of silver medals: John Woolcott (13 years), Nigel Power (11 years) and Peter Daw (10 years). Nigel Power continues to play a major role in the Guild today. A photograph on another page shows the recent membership surrounding the present parish priest. The list of social events and outings listed by "Mr. Mac" shows the Guild as an important part of parish life in addition to its members' work in serving the liturgy. Vocations to the priesthood have emerged from Guild membership. [P.1]

In February 1950 the Exeter Catholic Association was launched: its first Bulletin is mainly focussed on the maintenance of Catholic education facilities as evolved from the 1944 "R. A. Butler" Education Act. The Bulletin contains brief notices of forthcoming events both in Sacred Heart and Blessed Sacrament parishes. There are also notices of a Newman Association lecture in the University College (as it then was) and of a meeting under the auspices of the Student Christian Movement. Only one copy of the Bulletin has survived in the parish archives; it seems to have been a fore-runner of the 2004 publication "Making Links" which covers all Catholic activities in the Exeter District. The Exeter Catholic Association appears to have ceased activity at some time in the 1960s.

Fig 20   *The church choir in 1972 with Harold Stringer*

During a large part of the period under review in this chapter the choir was led by a remarkable organist, Harold Stringer, who had already attained to local fame as a cinema organist at the city ABC Cinema, where seated at the Wurlitzer keyboard he would rise from the bowels of the cinema to entertain patrons to music and accompanying slide shows. [5] His assumptions about the musical competence of those of us who were very much amateur choristers led to a few disasters, but under his conducting the choir managed to lead the congregation in a sung mass (including plain chant) every Sunday and to sing at the offertory a number of the better known motets. Harold Stringer left in 1975 after a difference of opinion with the parish priest. He died shortly afterwards.

On April 5th 1961 there was celebrated the centenary of the death of Dr. George Oliver, the pioneer of the restoration of Catholic worship from 1810, and the author of so many historical works. Bishop Cyril Restieaux of Plymouth sang pontifical high Mass in Sacred Heart Church and Dom John Stephan of Buckfast preached. [P.1] After lunch at the Rougemont Hotel there was a lecture by Dr. W.G. Hoskins on the life and works of Dr. Oliver. There was a very good attendance, showing the continued high esteem in which Dr. Oliver was held throughout the city and by the University College of the South West, in whose Gandy Street premises the Hoskins lecture was given. [P.13]

Two years later Pope John XXIII died on June 6th and a solemn requiem Mass was offered in Sacred Heart Church. It was attended by representatives of the other Exeter Christian churches and by the Mayor and civic party. [P.13] It was John XXIII who had set in motion the preparations for the Church's Twenty-first ecumenical Council, the first since Vatican I in 1869 - 70, [32] and it was that Council which defined papal infallibility. [79] The second Council opened on October 11th, 1962. Pope John was to live only nine months after opening the Council, and his successor, Pope Paul VI, carried through the work of what came to be known ever since as "Vatican II". [P.18, 38] By the time it closed on December 8th, 1965 it had produced documents and stimulated discussions which were to bring about many changes in the practices of the Church, whilst re-affirming the fundamentals of the Catholic faith. [P.18, 38]

The pages of the story of an individual Catholic parish (even when viewed in a wide context) are not the right place to analyse the many innovations and controversies occasioned by the follow-up to Vatican II. The documents emerging from the Council are sixteen in number and their texts run to over 100,000 words. [P.19] The "Dogmatic Constitutions" cover a range of topics fundamental to the practice of the Faith. They include the roles of bishops, priests, religious and the laity, the liturgy, ecumenism and education. References to the parish as a unit of the Church are to be found in several of the Dogmatic Constitutions. [P.19] Their conclusions are summarised in any case in the Catechism [36] to which reference has been made in the preface to this book. In the Constitution concerning bishops it is laid down that the parish "exists solely for the good of souls" and that parish priests are appointed only by bishops. Respect for local Rites in communion with Rome is emphasised in the Constitution on the Eastern Churches. The longest references to Parish functions are found in the Decree on the Apostolate of the Laity whose contents seem to re-emphasise what had already been said several times about co-operation between priests and people, about lay parishioners bringing Christian values into the rest of society, and about the parish being "a kind of a cell of a diocese". These sentiments also appear in the Dogmatic Constitution on the Church, especially in the Chapter IV on "the laity", whose apostolate is reiterated, though sometimes it appears in somewhat abstract, almost poetic, language.

We have no record of parish discussion groups or existing associations devoting specific sessions to the examination of the documents emanating from Vatican II, although there are references in several of the surviving weekly parish bulletins. It seems that the greatest popular impact of the new thinking on local parishes may have been felt in two aspects of parish life: liturgy and ecumenism. Pronouncements on the second of those subjects speak of non-Catholic Christians in a far more empathetic way than before. The emphasis in local parish discussion had been on tolerance and understanding, but also on other Christians "coming back to the church". However, prudence and humility now were the key-notes, and hasty expectations of unity were to be eschewed whilst common prayer had to underlie study and action. [P.18] Sacred Heart parishioners sought to respect that process in relation to their other Christian neighbours. [P.1, P.9, P.14]

It was in 1960 that a second Exeter example of building a "chapel of ease" church in a new housing estate was agreed on. The church of St. Bernadette in Galsworthy Square, Whipton was opened on October 5th that year. It followed a temporary Mass Centre in Polsloe Social Centre nearby. There was room in the church for 220 people to worship. It had a high tower and a piece of rock from the Lourdes grotto was built into the wall. [10] Unfortunately the envisaged congregation did not fully materialise, the demands upon a limited clergy became too great, local vandalism made the cost of maintenance prohibitive, and the church was demolished. [P.4, P.10]

It was in 1966 that Mass at Sacred Heart Church was first celebrated with the priest facing the people across the altar. A wooden altar had been constructed by Bernard O'Shaughenessy of the parish, whose skill in cabinet-making is evident in other church furnishings, including doors to the confessionals and the free-standing donation box at the back of the church. The first mass facing the people was celebrated by Monsignor Tobin with other priests as concelebrants, including the Provincial of the Marist Fathers and Fr. Frank Balment from Heavitree (as he then was). [P.1] There is no record of any open parish discussion of the new stance at Mass - now being introduced everywhere. The new arrangements seem to have been generally welcomed - or at least found acceptable. [P.20]

The liturgical changes involved both changed positions during Mass, a greater emphasis upon the use of English, the disuse of the nave pulpit and a reduction in the use of Latin. Interestingly, there had been discussion between the parish priest and the parish council on the best arrangement for the new altar. It was then thought possible to move the Boniface stone altar to the centre of the sanctuary, but the proposal was eventually dropped. [P.2, P.20]

A document produced in June 1970 by the Plymouth Diocesan Commission for Liturgy and Music (in the parish archives) contains a quotation from the Instruction on Music in the Sacred Liturgy, 5th March 1967: "Pastors of Souls should take care that besides the vernacular the faithful also can say or sing together in Latin those parts of the Ordinary of the Mass that concern them". The Plymouth Commission document goes on to distinguish between *rite* and *language*. The Proper of the Mass being variable is appropriately said in English , thus encouraging congregational participation. Even in the Ordinary of the Mass Latin may be used as appropriate. The people as well as the choir should be able to sing: the Responses, the Pater Noster, Credo III and "about one setting of the Kyrie, Gloria, Sanctus and Agnus Dei... It is also desirable that the people should likewise learn to sing in English those parts of the Ordinary and Proper that concern them". The Commission document also encourages the continued use of bells in the liturgy and the introduction of bidding prayers (then not yet formally introduced).

Understandably these changes led to some parishioners (not by any means only in Exeter) expressing strong opinions for and against them. The introduction of "new" liturgy with guitars and mass settings to popular sung tunes has earned enthusiastic support from some, whilst equally strongly others have favoured continued familiarity with Gregorian Plain Chant and long-established hymns. Sacred Heart parish has found a place for both, though different traditions have developed at Sunday masses, with all seeking common denominators at Easter and Christmas. The Mass of the 1962 rite is now celebrated once a month at Blessed Sacrament Church, Heavitree.

Two last comments sum up some of the discussion over the new liturgical practices as they have affected Sacred Heart parishioners. Eamon Duffy comments "The Second Vatican Council would dramatically change Catholic perceptions of the nature and force of tradition by harnessing the resources of the remote past liturgically and theologically, not as instruments of conservation but of change: the Council would sweep away precisely those external markers of what was often in fact relatively recent tradition". [23.3] Later in the same chapter of his book Duffy refers to the fact that the liturgical changes co-incided with a time of general challenge to authority in British society and that a misunderstanding (or even misrepresentation) of the place of tradition in liturgy led to a scramble away from all tradition in the name of "renewal". [23.3] In this connection Davie's analysis is also helpful. [19]

Fr. Cormac Rigby, whose collected sermons have a very wide circulation in the years since his retirement from the BBC, has a sharp reposte to an acquaintance "who was not born till after Vatican II and told me how really awful the Church was before the Council... no-one ever read the Bible, no-one could understand the Mass in Latin... The whole Church was run in fear and the Popes were triumphalist". Cormac Rigby sharply combats this false description by retorting: "The Catholics of 1950 loved the Church and the Mass every bit as much as you, if not more... How dare you be so snide about their faith?" [60]

On Sunday, June 15th 1958 during the annual procession at Sacred Heart a new Monstrance was used for the first time. It was given by the parishioners in thanksgiving that no-one was killed or injured when on Sunday, July 29th 1956, during the 9:30 am Mass there was a very fierce gale. At its height with thunder and lightening and torrential rain, the ornamental parapet of stone above the church porch came crashing down onto the street below. Fortunately no-one was passing at the time.

The first Parish Mass of Father Ivor Netto was celebrated on Saturday, March 31st 1973. His parents and relatives were joined by a large congregation. The concelebrants were Rev. Fathers D. Rossiter, G. Hay, H. Doyle and A. Cornish. Father Ivor gave his blessing to many after the mass, and all went to a reception and buffet at the Convent, Palace Gate. (P.1)

Sister St. Patrick of the Convent celebrated the Golden Jubilee of her religious profession on April 10th 1973, and concelebrated mass was offered that evening in thanksgiving by Fathers Balment (later Canon Balment), Coburg, Cornish, Doyle and Netto. The readers were Sister Mary Alfred and Sister St. Louis. At the Convent, after Mass, there was a large gathering of parishioners and other well-wishers. Sister St. Patrick was born in Exeter, the daughter of the late Mr. & Mrs. Frank Rivers of Mansfield Road, and went to Palace Gate Convent School as a pupil. On leaving school she worked for a while as a typist for Messrs. Kennaway, Wine & Spirit merchants in Palace Gate, before going to France to enter the Order of the Presentation of Mary at Bourg St. Andéol. (P.9)

At the University Service in Exeter Cathedral to mark the start of the academic year on Sunday, October 7th 1973 the preacher was Cardinal John Heenan, Archbishop of Westminster. He had been invited by the University and was accompanied in the Cathedral by the Dean. In that period the University Service was a formal affair with all the university staff and students in academic dress, who took part in a procession from the Guildhall to the Cathedral with the Mayor and Civic Party joining them. Miss Mary Dymond, a prominent Sacred Heart parishioner who was confined to a wheelchair in her last years, reported her delight at receiving an individual blessing from the Cardinal after the Cathedral Service. (P.1)

May 1974 saw the move of St. Nicholas School to Matford Lane where it was blessed and opened by Bishop Restieaux. September that year brought the national conference of the Saint Vincent de Paul Society to Exeter, with the Sacred Heart branch assuming major duties during its conduct in the University Great Hall. This included Pontifical High Mass. Bishop Restieaux in his welcome reminded his audience that "This diocese is the least Catholic part of England … it is truly missionary territory". (P.9)

The following year the national conference of the Catholic Women's League was held in the University Great Hall. As with the "S.V.P." the local section of the "C.W.L." had to be responsible for much of the hosting of a national event. The Catholic Women's League had brought their own national chaplain with them - Bishop Moverley of Leeds - but the Plymouth Diocesan Bishop and the parish priests of the Exeter parishes played a prominent part in the spiritual events of the Catholic Women's League transactions. (P.1) The C.W.L. had taken a step forward under the chairmanship of Sybil Hay to unite all three Exeter parish sections into one, to whose chair Elizabeth Leaper succeeded for the year of the National Conference. [P.9] The nineteen seventies seem to have thrust Exeter into the national Catholic limelight in many ways. More domestic concerns were also in evidence. On September 20th 1974 the Bishop presented "Mr. Mac." with the Bene Merenti Award in recognition of his years of work in altar serving.

April 13th 1976 was declared a National Day of Prayer for Peace in Northern Ireland. Services were held in Exeter Cathedral at the invitation of the Dean and Chapter. The Catholic contingent from Sacred Heart was prominent and the parish priest from Heavitree, Monsignor O'Neill, preached. Mass for Christian Unity in 1975 was attended by members of other city churches, and Canon Rice from Exeter Cathedral preached in Sacred Heart Church. He had already visited the church from the age of 3 with his aunt, and had later regularly attended benediction. [P.1]

In 1977 Councillor John Landers was elected Mayor of Exeter. On March 5th Pontifical Mass was sung in the presence of the Mayor and Mayoress, the Aldermen and members of the City Council. Joe O'Mahoney (late chairman of the Parish Council and a Knight of St. Columba) attended on the Mayor [P.1] In his daily work Joe guided tourists around Exeter.

The publication in 1979 of a Plymouth Diocesan Report, written by Fr. Bart Nannery and based on evidence obtained from 60 diocesan parishes, prepared us for the National Pastoral Congress in Liverpool in 1980. Robert Leaper attended the Congress as a Sacred Heart Parish delegate and gave a report back to the parish on the Sunday following, as well as writing an evaluation of the Congress in *The Tablet.* [42.2] *

Pope John Paul visited Britain in May 1982, among other things laying stress on its ecumenical content by visiting Canterbury Cathedral. Cardinal Basil Hume followed this up with a series of visits to Anglican services and to national ceremonies. He became president of the "Churches Together in England". He led a delegation from the Bishops' Conference to Rome to deal with the process of reception of former married Anglican clergy into the Catholic church as priests. [38] Sacred Heart parish has had the good fortune to benefit from the devoted service of a retired married former Anglican priest and his family. A number of parishioners journeyed to Cardiff for the nearest Rallying point to Exeter for the Papal visit. John Woolcott, active in Catholic youth work in Exeter for many years led a delegation to the Papal Youth Rally in Cardiff. [P.1] It is indeed remarkable that the visit of the Holy Father should have been given such a unanimous and enthusiastic welcome, and to have presented such an opportunity for Christian renewal and reconciliation.

---

* Compare Liverpool Pastoral Congress: The 25th Anniversary, Michael M. Winter; The Pastoral Review, May/June 2005.

In 1982 such a Mission of Renewal involved Sacred Heart parish with two other churches. The Reverend K. Hibberd, minister of Southernhay United Reformed Church preached at the evening service in the Sacred Heart Church, the first time for such an event. Another ecumenical initiative had been the "Central Exeter Chaplaincy" for those working in shops and offices in central Exeter. Seven ministers from five denominations participated, Fr. Keith Collins being the Catholic representative.

On Sunday, June 8th, 1980 "About 4,000 Roman Catholics from many parts of the South West made a pilgrimage to Exeter Cathedral for the first Sunday Mass to be celebrated there since the Reformation". [(P.15)] In these dramatic words the local press reported on the celebration by Bishop Cyril Restieaux of Mass to mark the thirteenth centenary of the birth of St. Boniface. The Dean and Chapter had made the cathedral available to the Roman Catholic communion and the Bishop of Exeter, Bishop Eric Mercer, and the Dean, the Very Reverend Clifford Chapman, were present for Mass. The Catholic Bishop of Portsmouth, Mgr. Anthony Emery gave a homily on St. Boniface and his significance for a time of greater ecumenical work. The Anglican Diocesan commemorative service for St. Boniface had been held in the morning of the same day. However, the saying of Mass in the Anglican Cathedral was indeed a dramatic step forward in denominational relationships. There was some objection to the event outside the Cathedral by the Reverend Joe West, who held aloft a placard proclaiming: "This Mass is a blasphemous fable". [(P.13)] The protest on behalf of the Exeter Reformed Independent Church was reported in the local press to have gained meagre support. The Right Reverend Phillip Pasterfield, Anglican Bishop of Crediton, pointed out that celebrations of St. Boniface's witness to the Christian faith had brought all Christians together. Some 50 young people, led by John Woolcott, had walked from Crediton to Exeter in pilgrimage to the Cathedral for the service. [(P.1, 67)]

There had been a partial precedent to the Cathedral Mass for St. Boniface earlier in 1980. The year marked the fifteenth centenary of the birth of St. Benedict. The Abbot and monks from Buckfast, at the invitation of the Dean and Chapter, came to Exeter Cathedral to sing Latin Vespers on March 28th. Many members of Sacred Heart parish joined in the Cathedral congregation, presided over by the Bishop of Exeter. [(P.1)]

1984 is best known in the English-speaking world for George Orwell's chilling political satire of that title. Happily for the parishioners of Sacred Heart, 1984 had quite a different significance. It was the year of the centenary of the opening of the church and a programme of events was successfully completed during the year. There was High Mass, at which the Bishop of Plymouth was the principal celebrant, on November 18th, the date on which the first mass was celebrated in 1884.

A brochure produced by a parish centenary committee lists the events of the year, the publication being well illustrated with photographs and with charming line drawings by Gillian Curran. The Garden Fete had a Victorian fancy dress parade;

Ron Tamplin and Charles Causley gave a poetry reading; the Pen-y-Darren Choir from South Wales gave concerts; Richard Dennis and Mr. Mac arranged a Flower Festival for three days during which the vestments used in the church were on display; there was a children's craft exhibition and a programme of Christmas readings and music. Perhaps the most ambitious promotion was a three-day performance of the medieval Chester Mystery Play with a cast of about one hundred drawn from parishioners of all ages from seven to seventy and with participants from six other Christian churches in the city - a truly ecumenical enterprise.

During these years the Manpower Services Commission, established by central government, ran special schemes aimed at reducing unemployment and helping people seeking work to learn new skills. The Sacred Heart Parish, and our neighbours the Baptist Church, ran schemes from which both churches benefited and as a result of which people learnt new skills and found jobs. At Sacred Heart the whole church floor was renewed and re-polished, and the sanctuary wooden mosaic flooring was re-laid.

A useful role in monitoring the state of the fabric in consultation with the parish priest, was played by Clem Yule during the reign of three parish priests - Canon Balment, Father Collins and Canon Jaffa. He resolutely tracked down leaks and damage, ensured drain clearance, and scolded parishioners who appeared to lack concern and appreciation of our heritage. Despite the labours of his predecessors, the present parish priest has had to undertake major roof and tower repairs and - particularly - to see that persistent leaks are successfully cured.

The year of the centenary saw Sacred Heart Parish in good shape, having renewed its dedication, refurbished its church interior, extended its ecumenical relations and prepared its parishioners without presumption for sixteen more years of a somewhat troubled twentieth century full of material change.

CHAPTER 9

<u>Education and Recreation</u>

The first Catholic school in Exeter since the Reformation was opened in Alphington by a Mr. Laurence Halloran in 1782. He was later ordained and returned to Exeter to live in the Mint where he died in 1852, and is reputed to be buried there. One of Mr. Halloran's pupils went on to train for the priesthood in Liège, Belgium, and eventually became provincial of the English Jesuits. [P.8] At the Mint Mission the decision to open a school was taken in 1854. Bishop Errington laid the foundation stone and the small school opened in 1855. [P.10] The venture was made possible by contributions from parishioners as well as the payment of fees by parents. Religious orders provided the teaching. Five years after the opening we find a note in Diocesan records of a Sister Mary Annunciata of the Franciscan Sisters resigning as she objected to teaching boys and girls of all ages in the same class. [P.10] By 1865 the Faithful Companions of Jesus (a renowned teaching order) had been invited by the Rev. K. Dupuy to ensure good teaching. A comment by Bishop Vaughan at the time is illuminating: "At Exeter the Faithful Companions of Jesus have been established where they will have charge of the poor schools and will teach a middle-class day school." (Advent Pastoral Letter 1865) [P.10]

In 1872 it was agreed by those in charge of the school that the older boys should be taught separately; this involved an expansion of premises. In November 1884 Bishop Graham blessed new premises for the school taken over from the chapel at the Mint.

In 1897 the Sisters of the Presentation of Mary came from France to teach in the Mint School, their arrival being negotiated by a Basilian priest, Père Aureille. After two years' training two sisters started teaching, and by the 1920s there were three sisters and a male teacher at the Mint.

It does not seem generally realised that the Mint school continued at the same location till as late as 1959 when it moved to former Anglican School premises in Holloway Street (now occupied by the Jehovah's Witnesses). Monsignor Tobin is recorded on February 18th that year as having blessed the school and rung the Angelus. As with most schools, the note-worthy occasions in the school calendar included special events occasioning school holidays. In 1910 the school flag (a gift from Mark Rowe & Sons) had been flown at half mast on the death of Edward VII; it was flown at full height on the subsequent proclamation of the accession of George V. During the First World War in 1917 a "Belgian School was opened at the Guild Room." [P.9]

As in the previous reigns, the school commemorated the death of one monarch and the proclamation of the succession of another: George V's funeral was in January

1936 and his son was proclaimed as Edward VIII six days earlier when his father died. This time there was a difference: Edward abdicated and his brother succeeded him as George VI. At the end of the same year St. Nicholas School in the Mint closed in honour of the enthronement of the Anglican Bishop of Exeter, Charles Edward Curzon.

In September 1939 the school closed for normal lessons, as did all other schools, but pupils had to report daily - with their gas masks - and prepared for air raid drill. In 1940 the school received evacuees from London. In May 1942 during the fire bomb raid the school was damaged and had to be closed for three months. The children were remembered by the Soroptomists in Toronto and by children in Rhodesia, both of whom sent presents. The school roll increased steadily in the 1950s and in June 1958 an exchange was arranged through the Local Education Authority with the premises in Holloway Street to which the school moved in February 1959. After much discussion of changes to the road system in central Exeter and a final meeting of all interested parties in January 1970, an agreement was reached through the Diocesan Trustees for a new St. Nicholas School to be built at Parkers Well on Matford Lane, having as close neighbours the School for Deaf Children and Central First School. St. Nicholas School opened in September 1973 with an enrolment of 334. The official opening by Bishop Cyril Restieaux and a range of civic dignitaries was on May 10th 1974. Sister Mary Alfred continued as Head after the move to new premises. The caretaker was Laurence McWilliam, "Mr. Mac." The school secretary was Agnes Storrie, later to be the unofficial guardian of St. Thomas of Canterbury Church on Dunsford Hill.

In the hundred and fifty years since its opening in the Mint St. Nicholas School has functioned in three locations: a fourth is now anticipated following Exeter schools re-organisation in 2005. Continuity has been maintained through the consistent identity and purpose of English Catholic education, wherever that education is located.

That continuity is expressed in one of the documents of Vatican II, the Declaration on Christian Education (Gravissimum Educationis). [P.20] The Declaration in fact deals only with fundamental principles of education and the role of the Church in the provision of it at all levels. It leaves the translation into practice to the Bishops in conjunction with those to whom the first and fundamental duty of upbringing is entrusted, the parents. It is also recognised that the Declaration must be applicable to widely different educational systems, as the State has played an increasingly interventionist role in educational provisions.

After a passage in which the role of teachers is given prominence, the Declaration states: "As for Catholic parents, the Council calls to mind their duty to entrust their children to Catholic schools, when and where this is possible, to support such schools to the extent of their ability, and to work along with them for the welfare of their children." [P.20] The extent and the form in which co-operation with other Christians is possible will depend upon very variable circumstances and systems, but the assertion of the rights of faith schools is very clear. In 2005 this is a matter of national debate, stimulated by the new situation of growing numbers of citizens of the Muslim faith. The educational response to these and other social changes will be clearly different in Catholic parishes in Exeter compared with those in its twin cities of Rennes, Bad Homburg and Terracina, each governed by distinct constitutional frameworks reflecting different political ideologies. Even in England alone there are clear regional differences.

The Plymouth Diocesan Yearbook for 2005 lists 37 voluntary aided schools with 9,510 pupils in the Catholic diocese of Plymouth; these include 4 secondary comprehensive schools. [P.4] There are listed in addition 6 independent (fee-paying) Catholic schools with 1360 pupils. In 2005 there is only one Catholic school in Exeter; that is St. Nicholas Catholic Combined School having in 2005 an enrolment of 350 children between three and eleven years old. [P.4] There are no secondary or independent Catholic schools. This contrasts with the situation in the 1960s in Exeter when there were three Catholic primary schools and two Catholic secondary schools (both fee-paying). Catholic nursery school provision has persisted, though being small in numbers catered for. Overall in Devon 98% of 3-4 year-olds access early education places. [25]

Fig 21 *Palace Gate Convent and School*

Catholic educational provisions in the Exeter area have mirrored to a large extent the history of religious orders in the Exeter parishes. Many of these orders have an explicitly teaching vocation. Their ability to continue with this vocational tradition depends upon a number of general trends which also affect parish life. "In 1968 there were almost 5,000 secular priests in England and Wales and 2,762 ordained male religious. 1998 statistics indicate just over 4,000 secular priests and 1,682 religious, with the age profile of serving priests steadily worsening; cobwebs gather in the corridors of the seminary extensions of the early 1960s." [23.3] There has been a reduction in Mass attendance, baptisms and marriages. Above all religious orders of the active or apostolic type have been heavily reduced. [19] Sacred Heart parish has not been exempt from the general trends throughout the country, though a remarkable degree of active engagement in parish societies persists. We are not concerned with a diagnosis of the causes for these trends at this point. It seems important, however, to record the facts, as seeking to evade them will lead to our being less effective and lacking in response to Christ's challenge, as Michael Hornsby-Smith has warned us. [32] As one of the more dramatic changes over the past thirty years has been the reduction in teaching activity by religious orders, the Exeter case merits sympathetic examination, coupled with appreciation for what has been achieved.

The situation of a voluntary denominational school like St. Nicholas school has been debated in public education bodies on many occasions. For example in 1923, when the school was still at the Mint, Exeter Elementary School Committee queried the admission to the school of three pupils who had moved out of Exeter to "a neighbouring South Devon town" (the town turned out to be Alphington). [P15] Their parents had sent them to St. Nicholas School "where the particular tenets of the Roman Catholic Church are taught." [P.15] Some members of the committee were reported as favouring some sanction against the school managers for ignoring the Elementary Schools Committee request that the children be educated in a Catholic school elsewhere (at the responsibility of the County Education Committee). Others of the local councillors bore in mind similar arrangements in Plymouth and favoured leaving the matter alone - primarily for the sake of the children.

On May 2nd 1923 Mr. Vincent Thompson (after whom an Exeter school was later named) argued that the case of the three children was a special one, that other Exeter children were excluded from the school, and that the wishes of parents should prevail in such a case. "Mr. Edgar Ware, as a Catholic layman, supported Mr. Thompson's resolution." [P.15] During the debate the secretary revealed that "the average cost of education was £11 per child, and £5 of that fell upon the rates." [P.15] By August 4th 1923 the Education Committee had decided to penalise the governors of St. Nicholas School for defiance of the committee by ceasing to maintain the school, that is by disclaiming liability for teachers' salaries and cost of maintenance.

The Catholic minority in Exeter had been most careful to respect local authority regulations and to be known as good citizens, but this controversy set the denominational school case in direct conflict with the elected local authority, and "matters of principle" were soon raised. An appeal to the Board of Education in London appears to have resolved the dispute in favour of admitting the three Alphington children to St. Nicholas School as a special case. [P.15] At this point

Fr. Barney entered the fray and in a letter published in the Daily Gazette on August 13 accused the newspaper columnist of bias in dealing with the Alphington Children dispute. The Devon County Council had refused responsibility for payment on the grounds that alternative schooling was available. Eventually the Exeter Committee allowed the children to remain at the school, and the City Education Committee "under protest" agreed to resume maintenance of St. Nicholas School. The Alphington question, however, caused general concern to all local education authorities, and the attention of the Association of LEAs was drawn to the case - and to its solution.

Fig 22   *The chapel at Palace Gate Convent School*

In 1938 the Presentation Sisters opened at Palace Gate a non-fee paying class for girls aged 11 to 14 ("St. Michaels") which was eventually in 1950 absorbed by Mount St. Mary's.

After the major national debates at the end of the Second World War, St. Nicholas School had to find its place under the 1944 (Butler) Education Act. [19] It became a voluntary aided school, a status which seems to have survived crises and to have prompted consistent support from the parishioners of Sacred Heart Church, their loyalty to the school being frequently invoked by clergy and school governors alike. [P.7] "The Catholic Church, unlike the Church of England, has benefited from the 1944 Education Act, seizing the opportunities offered to develop education and being more resolute in financing it." [51.2] After the pioneering headship of St. Nicholas School by Sister Maria Alfred when it was at the Mint, she continued as Head after the move to the new premises in Matford Lane in 1974. Her retirement was followed by the appointment of the first lay headmaster, Martin Bellis; he was succeeded in 1991 by Mathew Scott. [P.9, P.10] Sister Maria Alfred continued active as a prison visitor till her final retirement.

We turn now to the contents of the carefully preserved minute book of the meetings of the managers of St. Nicholas School from March 1956 to September 1998. [P.7] From the rich fund of evidence recorded over these forty two years it is difficult to select the most significant, but some common features do seem to emerge. First, and most significant for the Sacred Heart Parish, is the assumption that parish concerns include the support for, and consistent improvement of, St. Nicholas School. Late in the period in question this took shape in the publication of a "Making Links" newsletter linking all Exeter parishes with St. Nicholas School, and of course with one another. In various practical ways Sacred Heart parish groups helped the school children by providing transport for outings, by financing a variety of pieces of equipment, by celebrating First Holy Communion and Confirmation as sacraments celebrated in the parish church to the benefit of St. Nicholas School Children, their parents and their sponsors. [P.21]

A major pre-occupation of the governors/managers has been the enrolment of pupils. Numbers have had to be maintained to justify the school's continuation. In fact the demand for admission has remained high. "What is absolutely clear," writes Grace Davie, "is the popularity of church schools." [19] (She then speculates on the reasons for this). When the Diocesan Schools Commissioner, Mr. P. Blake, visited the Governors' meeting in February 1969 he furnished an outline statement on admission. The Governors agreed to give priority to Roman Catholic children, then to children of other Christian denominations, particularly with those having brothers or sisters at the school. The old question of admitting children from outside the school catchment area was reviewed several times. A letter from the Diocesan Bishop in March 1985 ruled that in a Catholic school of over 100 pupils not more than 30% should be non-Catholic. The question of defining eligible Catholic pupils has been the subject of much speculation. [17, 32, 38,80]

The managers appear to have spent a good deal of discussion and correspondence with the Director of Education's office, first for Exeter and later for Devon County, on a range of matters: teachers, premises and school transport. Most of these questions seem to have been amicably settled and relations seem to have been generally cordial.

A good deal of managers' time seems to have been invested in the appointment of staff. Whether the time spent is greater than in any comparable school is not clear. It may be that the combination of having relevant professional qualifications and also commitment to Catholic education objectives is an exacting one, both to those applying and those appointing to posts.

The availability of Catholic secondary education has been a recurrent theme in managers' discussions. This was first formally recorded in January 1963. Various possibilities for facilitating Catholic education after Primary stage have been mooted, involving the independent sector, the LEA and the central government department.

Though the school maintains its Catholic identity, the record shows that it joins with other schools in sports, competitions, celebrations and special ventures. It seems to have recorded success and enjoyment by pupils. Similarly many governors are themselves engaged in civic and voluntary association work.

The first lay manager to be elected chairman of governors was the then Mayor of Exeter, Patrick Spoerer in December 1964, assuming his duties as chairman in the following year. This marked a break with the seeming assumption that the parish priest chaired Governors' meetings. From the 1980s onwards chairmanship was assumed sequentially by clergy and by governors.

The degree of parish involvement in St. Nicholas School can be gauged from the direct engagement of parish priests and from the many governors who have undertaken other parish work either simultaneously or subsequently to their governors' appointments. Appreciative notes appear in the minutes for example to the work of Mrs. Cecilia O'Keefe as a teacher and of "Mr. Mac" as the devoted caretaker. Father Frank Balment features frequently in the minutes before and during his appointment as parish priest (Canon Balment died in 1987). Sister Sheila McCarthy was appointed as a teacher in 1974. Dorf Ruscoe, Elizabeth Leaper, John Woolcott and Joan Rees have been governors, Dr. Rees also giving voluntary service as an art teacher. Neville Simpson was appointed as clerk to the governors in 1985. He was succeeded by Susan Hills, Peter Geoghegan, Sheila Jones and Sara Tully.

A Parent-Teacher Association held its inaugural meeting in 1969, attended by 150 parents. This marked the beginning of closer and more structured involvement of parents and pre-dated later legislation in 1986 making it obligatory. In the Governors' report to parents in 2004 the current chairman, Nick Day, refers to the Parent-Governor Forum, a familiar and successful device for local involvement. In 2005 the Home-School-Parish Forum was revitalised to include the wider community and became the "School-Parish-Community Forum."

The School "Mission Statement" of 2004 makes explicit the school commitment to "the teaching and values of the Catholic Faith that is central in our daily lives." Clear support of the Governors for this assertion of purpose is exemplified by the work of the school chaplain, currently Sister Anna. It has always been implicit in the Governors' meeting records, particularly in March 1988 when Sister Sheila spoke on the subject.

Concern has often been expressed for the number of Catholic schoolchildren who do not persist in the practice of their faith after First Communion or Confirmation. "There has been extensive leakage, widespread abandonment of religious practice" wrote Watkin in 1957. [80] For comparison a similar plaint was raised in the report to the Exeter Anglican Diocesan Board of Education way back in 1840 which highlighted the essential role of schoolteachers in ensuring an attachment to Christian principles and practices after leaving school. Concern for this problem among the governors of St. Nicholas School is neither original nor easily solved. [19] * The reasons for it and the solutions to it are the subject of continued speculation and proposed programmes in all Christian churches. [P.20] The ultimate responsibility, it seems agreed, rests with parents. [32]

The Board of Governors is composed of a number of interested parties reflecting the governing Acts of Parliament concerning Voluntary Aided Schools, as distinct from Voluntary Controlled Schools of which most Anglican Schools are examples. What are called "Foundation Governors" nominated by the Diocesan Bishop are in the majority, balanced by parent representatives, and representatives of the local authorities. In 1985 the make-up of the Governors was made clear when at the conclusion of the term of office of the then governors a new set of Foundation governors was appointed. They together with the representatives of the local authorities, elected the parish priest as chairman, also appointing a clerk to the governors. From 1986 the school teaching staff have elected a Governor.

Other matters which have recurrently appeared in the minutes of Governors' meetings have been: Bus transport to school, including meeting the cost, maintenance of school buildings, relationships between governors and staff, making Governors' meetings open to parents, the celebration of Mass in the school on specific occasions, the finances of the school (with notable evidence from Fr. H. Doyle) resulting in the establishment of a "School Fund" in 1997, Health and Safety responsibilities (especially apparent from the 1990s onwards), and school uniforms.

In 1995 the school celebrated its centenary, and a suitable programme of events was organised, Mr. John Landers being the leader of the group arranging them. Incidentally the year marked 25 years of John Landers being a school governor.

---

* Fr. Bernard Hahesy of Plymouth is very critical of modern teaching of religion in Catholic schools in Britain (in his 2004 edition of "In defence of Catholic Teaching").

Also in this year Martin Overy retired as a parent governor but was re-appointed as a Foundation Governor and subsequently elected as chairman of the Board after Ed Channing's term of office.

The minutes book entries end at June 1998. Interviews with Martin Overy and his successor as chairman, Nick Day, do not reveal any major changes in the work of the governors as already outlined. There has been, however, considerable expansion in publicity and communication about the work of the school to parents, to concerned parishioners, to other Christian denominations. The appearance of "Making Links" and an expanded and enhanced annual report have played their part in this.

The concluding note must be of the announcement in 2004 of a re-organisation of schools in the Exeter area by the Education Authority. This has opened up the possibility of a new school building on a new site for St. Nicholas School. Public meetings were called by the governors at which alternative choices for change were outlined. After lively discussion it was agreed by an overwhelming majority of those at the general meetings, and subsequently agreed by the Governors, to pursue negotiations for a possible new St. Nicholas Primary School at Ringswell Avenue, Heavitree. If the negotiations are successful the move would not take place until September 2006 at the earliest. Exciting new prospects open up for the school which started life in a small building in the Mint a hundred and fifty years ago.

Meanwhile, what has been happening to the schools provision in the independent sector, for which the Presentation Sisters have long been responsible at Palace Gate, Mount St. Mary's and Rosary House? Reference has already been made in the St. Nicholas Governors' meeting in December 1995 to the possible implications for that school and its pupils of changes in Catholic education provisions elsewhere in Exeter.

The sisters of the Presentation of Mary (Castelgandolfo) have served in Exeter parishes since 1896. In compiling a brief account of their work here we have the advantage of their permission to consult their Annals which they have meticulously maintained since their arrival. There is also the published history of Mount St. Mary's School, and a shorter anonymous written account of Rosary House in the Mount St. Mary's library. I have been considerably helped by recent interviews with Sister Guy Marie Lamontagne and Sister Edward Mary Milsom and by personal evidence given by former pupils: Kathleen O'Shaughnesey, Shirley Ann Blaskett (née Ride), and Mary Genevieve Bownes (née Leaper).

The Congregation of Sisters was founded in 1796 by Marie Rivier who was apparently a person of small stature but powerful presence, who among her other attributes was said "to speak as well as a Jesuit." The first convent moved to Bourg-St.-Andéol in France in 1821 and the Order was known by that connection for many years. The Sisters were invited to Exeter through the instrumentality of Père Edouard Aureille, a Basilian priest who had served in Plymouth. Bishop Graham was seeking a religious order who would take on teaching duties in Exeter. The first sisters arrived in March 1896. They were welcomed at Exeter St. Davids station by Canon Hobson as parish priest and were found temporary lodging by a Miss Gifford "a fervent Irish Catholic" at 34, Richmond Road. "The damp climate" did not agree with the health of two sisters who were obliged to return to France. (P.9)

Canon Hobson, however, discussed with a Mr. Liddel the possibility of purchasing another house, and this was done when the premises on the north side of Palace Gate were occupied by the sisters on March 25th 1897. (This house is now part of Exeter Cathedral Choir School). The main drawback of those first premises was their lack of recreational grounds. The Annals record the Sisters' conclusion that parents were inflexible in their demand for playing fields. "The English show themselves quite firm on this point. Their first consideration in choosing an institution for their children's education is to ensure that they have space and open air" (Translation).

The large house and gardens opposite the Sisters' house came up for sale. Again the benevolent Mr. Liddel came to their aid. On April 5th 1897 the sisters moved into what had been the family residence of the Peters family. Mr. Liddel's two daughters were among their first pupils, whose numbers remained at a modest ten to fourteen for some time, but gradually increased up to the beginning of the First World War. "Protestant parents," we read in the Annals, "showed us every consideration; they do not hesitate to entrust their children to us, recognising that the education we give them is comprehensive and thorough." An entry in 1915, after the war had raged for a year, reads (in French) "At the start of the terrible war which still ravages our country, the house in Palace Gate has given shelter to many Belgian refugees; several families have found a home for weeks in our small "corner of St. Michael"…many of them have been looked after in the convent where they had some refreshments after hearing Mass. Now a dozen Belgian children still receive from us the benefit of a Christian education." More French and Canadian Presentation Sisters came to Exeter in 1916-17 despite the manifest problems of communication during the war. Sisters began to study for English teaching qualifications, and the Palace Gate school became well established and to have good exam results and good inspection reports. The sisters helped also in organising a retreat for the Children of Mary, one of which was held in September 1939: the date when several London evacuees came to the convent school. Swimming and hockey now featured on the school curriculum, to the great satisfaction of parents.

When war broke out again in 1939 the French and Canadian nuns opted to stay at their posts in England. "Mercifully the war has not harmed us much," runs an Annals entry in 1941, "The blessed Virgin has protected us." There were at that time 21 sisters at the Palace Gate Convent with 100 pupils. The Annals compare the experiences of their Sisters at the Plymouth convent who suffered a great deal more from the German air raids.

In April 1942 Exeter suffered a bombing raid during which the convent was damaged, as was the nearby Cathedral. The Annals give a vivid contemporary account of the fire-bomb blitz of May 1942 which is to be compared with that of Hoskins quoted in an earlier chapter.

Pressure on space at Palace Gate made the Order decide to expand elsewhere whilst still retaining the original premises and indeed purchasing two adjacent houses for the sisters and an extension to classrooms. In December 22nd, 1948 the sisters purchased Matford House, subsequently renamed Mount St. Mary's for use as a secondary school. [P.18] More sisters came from Bourg-St.-Andéol and more lay teachers were employed to help with the increased pupil enrolment. The new school was opened and blessed by Bishop Grimshaw on January 18th, 1949. One very visible change came to the sisters in 1967: their former all-black enveloping garments were changed to habits more akin to current customary female clothes, including less enveloping headdress. Photographs show how very striking, even perhaps intimidating, the earlier habits had been; one of our other Christian informants recalls how mysterious the nuns had originally looked to them.

During the three post-war decades the religious community (including girl pupils) attended mass in the Palace Gate chapel (of which a photograph has survived) and also in the lovely chapel still used at the building now lived in by the nuns at Mount St. Mary's (Matford House). However, the sisters also regularly attended mass, especially those said on special occasions such as First Communion at the Sacred Heart Church, one of them for some time acting as sacristan. Parishioners regularly used the Palace Gate premises for Parish Garden Fetes in the convent grounds, and for meetings in the large gymnasium hall. The proximity of church and convent was a great boon to parishioners.

A small number (the records are no more precise than that) of boarders were taken at Palace Gate Convent, some as young as 8 and 9 years old. While most of their memories are happy ones, it seems to have been a life with few concessions to youth, and an expectation of falling in with the routine of a convent. The lovely garden to the rear of the convent school, sweeping up to the old city wall, was much appreciated, and one "old girl" remembers collecting bags of conkers there.

As with the children of St. Nicholas School, the convent school children participated in many Exeter events with other schools - sports, musical, drama. Sister Edward Mary accepted an invitation to read the lesson at the Harvest Festival at St. Lukes in October 1976, which is one good example of the integration of the nuns into the life of the city. A crucifix was given to St. Margaret's School in Exeter by Mount St. Mary's School when it closed - a gesture commented on most favourably by St. Margaret's staff.

The expansion of primary schooling and the demand from the locality of Heavitree led the Order to establish a private primary school at Rosary House, adjacent to Blessed Sacrament Church in Heavitree. This provision lasted until 1985 when demand seems to have declined and the Primary School there was closed. Infant school provision remained until 1996 at Palace Gate.

As well as their teaching obligations it should not be forgotten that the Order of Presentation of Mary is also pledged to a life of prayer and study. Moreover, their parish integration already mentioned, implies participation in a range of social and celebratory parish events. These include their share in running the Catechetical Summer Camps for parish children. Sister Saint Patrick's example is striking in that connection. Always active in parish social life, she joined in the parish outing to Arlington Court on August 27th, 1979. Two days later she had a massive stroke and died in Southernhay Hospital, surrounded by her Sisters. She had been baptised, confirmed, made her First Communion and played the harmonium - all at Sacred Heart Church. Among the records of service in Exeter by the Presentation Sisters two more may be cited. Sister Sheila McCarthy was born in Exeter and joined the Order here. She was appointed a teacher at St. Nicholas School in 1974 and retired in 2000. She has recently devoted her energies to visiting the sick, including those in hospital. Sister Edward Mary Milsom came to Exeter in 1938, since when she has studied at Exeter University, taught at Palace Gate and Mount St. Mary's, at both of which schools she has had a successful spell as Head. Since her retirement she has lived at Mount St. Mary's and in 2005 decided to migrate to a convent of the Order in the United States of America. Among those saddened by her migration are Exeter City Football Club, of which she has been an ardent supporter.

The entries in the Annals had been in French since the sisters' arrival in Exeter. From 1991 onwards the entries were recorded in English, and this acknowledgment of the appropriate vernacular seems further evidence of integration into the locality and of openness towards the world outside the convent walls.

The Centenary of the Sisters' teaching services in February 1996 was unfortunately to be followed later in the same year by a decision to close the school. A High Mass of thanksgiving for the achievement over the years was celebrated in Sacred Heart Church on February 3rd, 1996. For a short time Mount St. Mary's had taken over a nearby property at 25, Lyndhurst Road. It was rented to the Catholic Children's Society, but was sold by the Convent in 1997. (P.9)

Catholic Secondary Education for boys had been provided since 1948 by the Marist Fathers at Winslade Park, about three miles out of Exeter City. It was an independent boarding and day school. Financial and recruitment difficulties led the Marist Order to decide to close the school and sell off the premises in 1972. This left the Exeter area with no Catholic secondary school for boys, which caused expressions of dismay among Catholic parents. Fr. Frank Balment (as he then was) called together a group of interested parents, including Professor Dominik Lasok and Mr. Ron Tamplin of Exeter University, to discuss ways and means of obtaining a Catholic comprehensive school for the Exeter area. The group sought the support of the parish priest and parishioners of Blessed Sacrament Parish, Heavitree and received support in principle but expression of scepticism about attaining the required potential for the possible establishment of a joint school with the Anglican Church (as had been done in the Torquay area). The chairman of the St. Nicholas

Parent-Teacher Association, James Chapman, was one of those pressing for action towards a joint Christian school. He made a strong intervention at the 1983 Parish Council Annual General Meeting. However, when the merger of Bishop Blackall and Hele School was achieved at the time of local authority re-organisation, the notion of Catholic interests being included did not find favour and the proposal had to be dropped. [P.2] At the time of the 1997 General Election there was discussion of a possible Catholic grant maintained school, but that was refused after the election.

The end of the Mount St. Mary School story came in 1997 and it has to be considered in the context of the world situation facing the Presentation of Mary Order. The well-known sharp decline in vocations (already noted), the need to rationalise their commitment, and the fact that the Order was subsidising Mount St. Mary's school by treating it as a "mission" commitment all pointed to the stark choice of ending the life of the school which - despite the apparent excellence of its standards - had received in 1995/6 less than 50% of its 1991 income, although fees had been increased. A number of alternatives were touted, including moving Palace Gate school to Wonford Road. Eventually the hard decision was taken by the Order to pull out altogether from teaching provisions in Exeter, to sell off the Palace Gate premises in toto and to dispose of the majority of the Wonford Road property. The Palace Gate property was sold to a developer who transformed the main buildings into flats and the teaching extension hall became the Brazz restaurant. The solution at Mount St. Mary's was to retain the Wonford House as the sisters' residence, to complete negotiations with the diocese for the use of the newer science building and to arrange with a small private school to buy the remaining structure. [P.9] (The inauguration of the Newman Centre in the former science building is described in the final chapter). The end result of all these developments is that since 1997 there has been no Catholic secondary school provision in the Exeter area.

Parish-sponsored recreational activities have always been on Sacred Heart parish agenda. Perhaps the most specifically Catholic in intent was the Exeter Catholic Youth Club opening in 1965 and inspired, and for a great part sustained, by John Woolcott. The Youth Club premises, known as the Loft, run in partnership with the Local Education Authority provided recreational pursuits, both indoor and outdoor, for some thirty to forty young people. In its report on "The First Five Years" the club received warm commendation not only from members but from spokesmen for the LEA, priests of the two Exeter parishes, Fr. Michael Murphy, Councillor John Landers, Mrs. Sybil Hay and Sister Sheila, the latter three being members of the Management Committee. The club continued successfully for years, but did not survive the much mourned death of John Woolcott in 1995, whose esteem was clearly displayed by the huge attendance at his requiem Mass in Sacred Heart Church. [P.1]

The Children of Mary were active in the 1930s in particular, producing an ambitious drama "Fabiola" in 1937 and several musical productions later. In the inter-war years and in the 1960s there were Catholic Scouts and Guides groups with Fr. George Hay as their chaplain. More recently there have been - and still are -

organised parish outings to Torquay pantomimes, to historic buildings, to pilgrimage sites, and for example to Salisbury and to Truro and Falmouth. Martin and Monica Overy have given a lead in encouraging Catholic social life among parishioners, supported by the Parish Pastoral Council. The provision of refreshments in the Lower Room after week-end Masses has helped parishioners to meet socially and has integrated many newcomers - thanks to the Catholic Womens' League. [P.2]

The considerable growth of formation courses available through the diocesan commission provisions at Cardinal Newman House has been modestly supplemented by the setting up of a small lending library at the back of the church. It was established by Ron Tamplin and sustained effectively by Hilda Swinburne, whose name has already been noted in connection with the Newman Association.

Supported consistently for the past twenty five years has been the work of the Catholic Children's Society, which as a Diocesan body provides care for children needing a family life. The Society faced a financial crisis in 1991. The chairman and directors were able to negotiate a "joint venture" with the Anglican Children's Society through the late Archdeacon John Richards; the successful conclusion was celebrated by a joint service in Sacred Heart Church in September 1992, presided over by the Catholic and Anglican Bishops. The experience of the joint venture was not without its traumas, but from it have developed new forms of child care and adoption culminating in "Families for Children," as an independent venture with a proven professional record and devoted voluntary family help. A collection in support of the Catholic Children's Society is appropriately taken at the Christmas crib in the church. A programme of links between schools and Children's Society workers is now being developed, and a new project called "Patchwork" supports parents in facing their vital family tasks.

Looking to the future, two stages of the social lives of parishioners will need renewed attention as successors to social groups which have lapsed over the last few years - young school-leavers as always, and the demographically increasingly important stage of later life. The former Senior Citizens Club ceased operations in the 1980s. Many parishioners in later life have patronised the Baptist Church social facilities or joined a body like Age Concern. Whether any specifically Catholic provision should be renewed remains for further discussion in the parish.

Fig 23 *St. Thomas of Canterbury Church, Dunsford Road*

CHAPTER 10

The Twenty-First Century

A final chapter is an opportunity to suggest some of the main pre-occupations of parishioners since 1984 and to speculate on what lies immediately ahead, and in the longer term, for Sacred Heart Parish.

"The Church is both a spiritual communion, whose members are bound together by their faith and love as disciples of Jesus Christ, and a visible institution, a worldwide body with an organisational framework of law and practice of bishops and dioceses, schools and parishes. It has the characteristics of both an extended spiritual family and of a highly organised society, and these are mutually supportive."[14] This vision of our purposeful working together in the parish has certainly been before parishioners' eyes, and has been emphasised by the clergy serving and leading the parish. Our multifarious activities have to be seen in that context. "Our duty is to dedicate ourselves with an earnest will and without fear to that work which our era demands of us, thus pursuing the path which the Church has followed for 20 centuries."[36.1] In reviewing parish achievements the following comment was offered by the Bishops of England and Wales in a 2004 publication: "The life of many parishes has been invigorated by individuals and families who have given their time to building up the local Church as an open and effective community."[14]

"Holy Mass needs to be set at the centre of the Christian life and celebrated in a dignified manner by every community, in accordance with established norms, with the participation of the assembly, with the presence of the ministers who carry out their assigned tasks, and with a serious concern that singing and liturgical music be suitably 'sacred'."[36.3] This guidance from Pope John Paul II is reflected in many recent developments in Sacred Heart Parish.

The office of permanent deacon has been revived and the role developed more specifically. The late Frank Bick was ordained Deacon in September 1985 and was followed by Delian Bower whose ordination to the permanent diaconate was on August 18th, 1999. Fr. Michael Koppel (one time at Sacred Heart Church) as Director of Permanent Deacons for Plymouth Diocese records that there are now "upwards of twenty of them ministering in parishes all over the diocese" and that they have a Deacons' Forum at diocesan level. Their functions include "Pastoral work in the parish and community; proclaiming and preaching the Gospel; and assisting at the liturgy, particularly the Eucharist." "Let all Deacons then," proclaims the Papal Congregation of Divine Worship, "do their part so that the sacred liturgy will be celebrated according to the forms of the duly approved liturgical books."[36.2]

"The only minister who can confect the Sacrament of the Eucharist in persona Christi is a validly ordained priest... However, if sacred ministers are lacking lay members of Christ's faithful may supply for certain liturgical offices according to the norm of law... Only out of true necessity is there to be recourse to the assistance of extraordinary ministers in the celebration of the liturgy... The extraordinary ministers of Holy Communion may administer Communion only when the priest and deacon are lacking, when the priest is prevented by weakness or advanced age or some other genuine reason, or when the number of the faithful coming to Communion is so great that the celebration of the Mass would be unduly prolonged."[36.2] The foregoing guidance from an Instruction of the Papal Congregation for Divine Worship has been followed at Sacred Heart parish church since the first "extraordinary ministers" were appointed by parish priests starting in the 1970s.[P.1, P.21] The first to be appointed was Laurence MacWilliam in 1975. In 1978 the next were Sister Noella, Frank Bick, John Woolcott, Neville Simpson and Fred O'Keefe. The number has increased, and there is now a rota of 21 "extraordinary ministers" assisting the priests and deacon at Mass or in taking Holy Communion from Mass to hospital, nursing and residential Homes and to parishioners who are house-bound. There does not appear to have been any confusion between the role of ordained clergy and the assistance of "extraordinary ministers" of Holy Communion: indeed their supplementing role has enabled more parishioners to maintain contact with the church and has facilitated their participation in the sacrament. Their help has been the subject of appreciative comment by beneficiaries in the parish.

With greater demands upon the clergy and a reduction in the number of clergy available in this, as in other, parishes the development of the role of "extraordinary ministers" in harmony with the functions reserved for ordained clergy will surely remain. (It might be wise also in view of the present linguistic ambiguity to review the use of the word "extraordinary" in this context and to find an epithet translated from the original text which accords more happily with current English usage.) The Year 2004-2005 is an appropriate time to pray and discuss this future development, being the year inaugurated as the "Year of the Eucharist" in a special apostolic letter, which also gives other guidance on the celebration of the Eucharist.[36.3]

A variety of subsidiary but important functions in the parish are directly related to the Mass. The role of Sacristan involves such tasks as preparing the hosts, dealing with liturgical linen, recording requests for Mass intentions by parishioners and ensuring the availability of the missals and other books as the priest and deacon require them. This function has since 1990 been performed most effectively by Gillian Bemrose.

We have already dealt with the work of the Guild of St. Stephen in Sacred Heart Parish. It is a work specifically singled out for praise in the Papal "Instruction" which also states that "Girls or women may also be admitted to this service of the altar at the discretion of the diocesan Bishop and in observance of the established norms."[36.2] Clearly recruitment to the ranks of altar servers will need continued parish support and encouragement.

An innovation in the parish over the past thirty years has been the introduction of lay readers, appointed by the parish priest from among those having some ability in this particular function. Clearly the proclamation of the gospel, "the high point of the Liturgy of the Word," is reserved to an ordained minister.[36.3] Other readings during Mass, or the recitals of the bidding prayers, introduced and concluded by the priest, are given by the Deacon or in turn by one or two on the rota of lay readers. The same applies to seasonal celebrations such as the readings and carols immediately before Midnight Mass at Christmas or the readings within the liturgy on Holy Saturday. The recruitment to the readers' rota and the provision of occasional training and review of experience in proclaiming the "word of the Lord" will demand attention, including the recruitment of new and younger readers. "It is Christ himself who speaks when the Holy Scriptures are read in church."[36.3]

There has been no relaxation in the obligation of Catholics to join in the celebration of Mass on Sundays.[20, 36.1, 36.3] Yet the numbers of those attending Mass has been falling and the general secularisation of Sunday is symbolised by the increased practice of shopping on Sundays which has had a marked impact on South Street and the whole central city area.

The records of Sacred Heart parish and those of Plymouth Catholic Diocese may be supplemented by reports from the Pastoral Research Centre, Taunton, directed by A.E.C.W. Spencer. In a publication in 2004 the Centre reports that between 1958 and 2002 in England as a whole:

- Parish clergy reported an overall increase in the "Catholic population" of 16%.
- Baptisms for infants under 1 year: fell by 61%.
- Late baptisms (age 1 to 13): increased by 191%.
- Sunday Mass attendance: fell by 49%.

In Sacred Heart parish between 1958 and 1962 baptisms rose from 56 to 72, and over the same period the "Catholic population" declined from 1304 to 1208. In 2005 it is estimated to stand at 1500. Age groups within parish populations are not given, but there is no evidence to suggest that the ageing process is markedly different among Catholics from that in the rest of the population, although birth-rates may be. This may all imply that parish work with children and young people is fully justified but has to be balanced by concern, and provision, for the later phases of parishioners' lives.[56]

Spencer speculates on the considerable rise in "late baptisms": could it be correlated with applications for entry to primary and secondary school? The 50% fall in Sunday Mass attendance nationally over the period in question has already been reported in many other relevant research studies on most Christian denominations in Britain, Ireland and elsewhere in Europe.[P.4, 18, 19, 23.3, 32, 51]

Spencer also queries how reliable estimates of the "Catholic population" really are. Consultation with the Diocesan Records Office suggests that there are many shrewd guesses involved, and that this item from Diocesan returns from parishes is a comparatively new one in any case.[P.10] The significance of the changes noted is, of course, a matter for open debate and for remedial action where appropriate. It would seem to be, however, an inadequate response in any parish to evade the issues posed by them or to suggest that unpalatable facts are insignificant. They may imply some adjustment in the places and times of Masses, and decisions about the form of service on occasions when it may be impossible to celebrate Mass. The Mass remains the fundamental and essential celebration of worship for which Sacred Heart parish has so far almost always had a priest available, but parishioners have come to recognise the inevitable and universal process of ageing in parishioners and priests.[P.2, P.10, 23.3, 56] Part of the response has been to pray for, and otherwise help towards, more vocations to the priesthood.

There are numerous group devotions in which parishioners take part - diocesan pilgrimages and devotions within the parish. Each year a contingent from Exeter joins in one of the Diocesan pilgrimages to Lourdes, for Youth of the Diocese, for handicapped children or for pilgrims in general.[P.4] In addition, Michael Olivant has organised pilgrimages to, for example, Fatima and Knock.

There are two devotions in which a group of dedicated parishioners take part every week-day. The morning prayer group meets before Mass at 9:45 and the Rosary group after Mass assembles before the Lady Altar. "This traditional prayer, so highly recommended by the Magisterium and so dear to the People of God, has a markedly biblical and evangelical character… and how could the mysteries of light not culminate in the Holy Eucharist?" [36.3]

During the two decades up to 2005 there have been many successful concerts and drama productions in the church. The 1983 production of the Chester Mystery Play may have been rather too ambitious to try again for some years, but it was followed by a Passion Play some years later. The young parishioners' group have produced shorter plays telling the Nativity of Christ story and there have been Music and Verse shows on a spiritual theme. These good examples of parish enterprise may spur on to greater endeavour present and future parishioners.

It was during Canon Bernard Jaffa's term as parish priest that noteworthy repairs to the fabric and improvements to lighting were carried out. These included the installation of the "Jaffa Gate" in 1989, allowing controlled access to the church by the side door, plus an alarm system. A small repository was installed which has proved a welcome facility for the purchase of religious goods of all kinds as well as ensuring that the church is open for private prayer at extended times. It is manned by a rota of volunteers headed by Margaret Langdon; continued recruitment to that team is a matter for review and an opportunity for service by those suited to the work.

Fig 24 *A cheque towards the cost of roof repairs - Fr. Bernard Jaffa, 1988*

A theme running through the parish story has been the involvement of parishioners with the public authorities now responsible for a wide range of services, especially in health, education and social care. Our local concerns are reflected in the 2001 Bishops' Conference introduction to "Participation & Partnership." Discussion between parish priest and parishioners and reviews of changing public authority practice has been ongoing, particularly in for example the functioning of the chaplaincy in the local hospital, in the complementarity of the work of volunteers and family carers with that of local authority social workers or the staff of nursing and care homes. In all these reviews of current and developing practice the parish has been fortunate in being able to draw upon the experience of parishioners who are architects, accountants, lawyers, doctors, nurses, social workers, consultants to health and local authorities, elected politicians or the elected officers of voluntary bodies. With due respect for vital professional confidentiality, this important human resource will no doubt continue to prove its worth to those needing help and will also serve to spread greater participation among parishioners. This may involve parishioners speaking out on "some fundamental moral issues relating to the moral and spiritual well-being of the human person in society, especially those issues touching the value and protection of human life."[14] The frequent appearance on the table at the rear of the church of petitions or submissions on questions such as abortion, euthanasia, child care, or - separately - solidarity with those in other countries suffering from civil war, famine or unjust economies shows an effort to accept responsibility as Christian citizens which has to be unremittingly renewed.[14, 35] "The follower of Christ is not pliant and cowardly, but loyal and strong."[P.21]

Changes in local government in 1974 and developments in health service administration in more recent years have had to be taken into account. The hitherto separate village of Topsham was annexed to Exeter in 1966 and the enlarged Exeter City Council sought unitary authority status under local government reorganisation in the 1990s - but without success, leaving Devon County Council with important functions in Exeter.[33.3] Interestingly Topsham has retained a separate Catholic parish which has well developed its own structure of parishioner involvement with the parish priest in both the liturgy and citizen concerns. The first chairman of the Diocesan Pastoral Council, Professor Margaret Green, is a Topsham Holy Cross parishioner. Allowing for an increased tendency to mobility in places of worship as already noted, Topsham is geographically, occupationally and traditionally more of a self-contained "community" than other Exeter localities.[33.3, 41.1, 81] Topsham is not dealt with as part of Exeter in all local history publications (except Hoskins [33.1]) and it has its own flourishing local museum. Much of its architecture reflects its past history as a port for Exeter.

Bodies such as the Devon Strategic Partnership, chaired by the Bishop of Exeter, and the Exeter Vision Partnership, an advisory group to Exeter City Council, are influential in policy decisions by those two executive elected bodies. Parishioners are to be found among the membership of both and the parish needs to be kept informed of their activities and to make representations when needs be. The consultative bodies mentioned are now part of a widespread programme of consultation on a wide range of executive bodies in public services of which any alert parish will need to take account. [18, 23.3, 25]

Meanwhile the physical environment of the parish and its church continues to change. There is since 2004 a rash of new building in central Exeter at a rate unprecedented in recent history.[12] Exeter's total population has been estimated to have risen by about ten per cent over the decade up to 2004. There have been changes in population structure in nearby districts, and more settlement is envisaged to the east of the city boundaries.[25] As has happened in the past, Sacred Heart parish is likely to add to its numbers more people of different cultural backgrounds from those settled here since 1950 or before.

Fig 25 *Altar servers with Monsignor Harry Doyle, 2000*

In all three Exeter Catholic parishes the amount of participation in parish activity groups is impressive. When Palace Gate Convent closed in 1996 a resource made available by the Sisters of the Presentation of Mary was no longer at parishioners' disposal. There had been a long tradition of meetings, concerts and garden fetes by Sacred Heart parish in Palace Gate Convent close to the parish church.[P.9] The small "lower room" meeting place in the presbytery building, though useful, is too small for gatherings of over 30 people. Fortunately negotiations between the Presentation Sisters, the Diocese of Plymouth, and the Parish Priest of Sacred Heart Church concluded with Cardinal Newman House in Wonford Road being established partly for diocesan use and partly as the Sacred Heart Parish Pastoral Centre.[P.10] Despite some initial criticism of its distance from South Street it has been very well used by both parish groups and other organisations seeking meeting places. The Centre's third annual report records that, during the year ending in June 2004, 395 separate parish activities used the Centre and that moreover there were 375 lettings to outside bodies, including Devon County Council. Blessed Sacrament parish is reported to be making increasing use of the Centre and to be contributing to the financing of joint activities such as RCIA and First Communion preparation. The financial state of the Centre is reasonably buoyant, though prudent provision has to be made for repairs, maintenance and redecoration. Overall governance of the Centre is assured by a parish group, including the parish priest, under the chairmanship of Nick Day. Philippa Day is Centre Co-ordinator and Ron Malins caretaker. Clearly the continued use and further development of this valuable facility will be reviewed and further supported over the next few years. Parish appointments, readers, extraordinary ministers of Holy Communion, Pastoral Council members and parish organisations are listed in appendix E. Details, of course, will change over time. The functions of "extraordinary ministers of Holy Communion" are laid down in "Redemptionis Sacramentum," an instruction of the Congregation of Divine Worship, 2004 - paragraphs 149 - 153.

Quite a different category of parish workers are those responsible for the care of the presbytery and of those who live there. The work was performed for many years from 1854 till 1981 by a succession of resident housekeepers. On the retirement of Miss Margaret Potts in 1981 the work has been done by visiting housekeepers. They are a vital part of parish life and many parishioners recall their helpfulness and support, and in some cases their zeal in guarding the presbytery.

An internal debate in the parish focuses on the choice of music for the celebration of the liturgy. This is paralleled by discussions and variable practices in other Christian churches. Discussion on the Parish Pastoral Council has identified a general desire to share musical expression particularly at Easter and Christmas. In the longer term at Sunday Masses two possible solutions to the different choices of music have been mooted: Those who prefer music in the contemporary idiom led by a group of instrumentalists will participate in the Mass where that is played, and those who prefer music led by an organist and choir with more emphasis on longer-established musical idiom will attend another Mass. The other solution would be to make an effort through continuing amiable discussions, led through the Parish Parochial Council with the parish clergy, to have some of each type of music at all Masses.

The debate needs to take account of: modern composers like Karl Jenkins pointing out the error of musical categorisation; a genuine opportunity for young parishioners to choose through open access to all music and not to be excluded from learning about for example Gregorian Plain Chant; a willingness by all to listen to modern composers from Britain and elsewhere; the call to respect "the pride of place given to Gregorian Chant...but also other sacred music, especially polyphony" as stated in Vatican II document on sacred music in the liturgy [21], and in the 2004 Instruction on the Holy Eucharist. "In the Sunday celebration there should be true and suitable sacred music." [36.2] Lastly in "Abide With Us," inaugurating the year of the Eucharist 2004-5, we read "for a serious concern that singing and liturgical music be suitably 'sacred'." [36.3] The ways in which Sacred Heart parish can participate in the practice of eucharistic adoration outside Mass in 2004-5 in particular have been reviewed on the Parish Pastoral Council. These have included the revival of Benediction and the "Holy Hour" on Sunday afternoon. They also included concern for reverence for the Blessed Sacrament in the tabernacle, which appears in some cases to have changed over recent years. [P.2]

Membership of a Christian church transcends classifications such as class, race or nationality. Even more fundamentally and universally "Every form of social or cultural discrimination in fundamental personal rights on the grounds of sex, race, colour, social condition, language or religion must be curbed and eradicated as incompatible with God's design." [36.1] Even in Humanist thinking the categorisation of humankind based on ethnic or other wide groupings is now discredited [46], though differentiation in God-given talents is evident. [36.1] Hence the celebration of cultural diversity and mutual respect is to be promoted but emphasis upon single factors like ethnic origin may lead to blunders like the assumption of homogeneity where there are in fact wide differences in any one ethnic grouping. These are among the issues recently reviewed by the Diocesan Justice and Peace group. [P.4]

Within European nationalities who have worked and worshipped together in Exeter, one thinks of fellow Catholics from Ireland, especially the crucial contribution of many priests, but also that of many doctors and nurses. In listing priests serving Sacred Heart parish since 1934 Monsignor Doyle identified twelve of them of Irish background, many coming here to the English Mission. Those who wish to continue the celebration of St. Patrick's Day and remember a cultural heritage are respected by fellow parishioners of different backgrounds.

One thinks too of parishioners originally of Polish culture settling in Devon, particularly as ex-service men after World War II or due to professional engagement in the area. The late Professor Dominick Lasok Q.C. made a distinctive contribution to the parish, and his family have been prominent in parish activities. Mr. Joe Prywata has been well known for his roles as altar server and extraordinary minister of Holy Communion. In considering how best to welcome newcomers and to engage with them in open-minded discussion about adjustments that may have to be made reciprocally, Sacred Heart parish has some useful precedents on which to draw, and it seems wise to think ahead as to how to apply them to ensure harmony in parish diversity. [14, 18, 19, 32]

The Parish Pastoral Council made a survey of parish opinion in 2000 which gave some indication of parishioners' priorities. Opinions about the liturgy as currently carried out were equally divided, there being three times as many positives about the music as there were negatives. The church building evoked 43 positive and 20 negative responses (the latter including complaints about roof repairs). Unanimous were positive opinions of the friendly and welcoming attitude of clergy and parishioners. There were few opinions expressed about St. Nicholas School and the children's liturgy but those responding were entirely positive. Rather less favourable were opinions about opportunities to learn more about the faith - 23 negatives to 1 positive. The parish team was viewed positively by almost all respondents and a majority of 69 to 13 considered the feeling of "community" to be a "plus." Perhaps surprisingly 38 expressed negative opinions about the social life of the parish and 29 about communications within the parish.

When asked what they did not like about the parish and what they would like changed there was a wide range of replies, those gaining most negative notes being "Nothing" and "The heating!" The clergy and the Parish team featured high on the positive list of all Mass attenders. Lastly as many as 136 respondents, fairly evenly spread over all Masses, stated that they belonged to no parish group or organisation. Whilst recognising that this might merely be a legitimate free choice for some parishioners, the Parish Pastoral Council responded by seeking to engage the 74 respondents who said they would be interested in becoming more involved in the parish. It resulted in only 3 parishioners being further engaged! These soundings of parish opinion provide enough data on which to build by both clergy and the Parish Pastoral Council. To what extent will they form the continuing agenda for action in the coming years?

When we come to parish connections with education at university level we can draw on a report from the Catholic chaplain, Canon Paul Cummins, who in 2003 wrote as follows:

"**Exeter University Catholic Chaplaincy** was established in the 1960's. We have a large house with a flat for the Chaplain, a self-contained flat and four bed-sits, which are rented out to students. The Chaplaincy building also has a chapel, a fully licensed bar, a library, two offices and two meeting rooms. The meeting rooms are used extensively for a variety of events by such groups as: the Catholic Society, Christian Union, the Ecumenical Team, Inter-Faith groups, local Anglican groups, counselling training courses, Diocesan in-service training sessions.

The liturgical activity at the Chaplaincy is centred on the celebration of the Sunday mass, which is lively and well attended.

The Ecumenical Chaplaincy Team are committed to working together wherever possible, and work alongside the university support services for the pastoral support of the students. There is also a Staff Christian Network who meet occasionally at the Chaplaincy.

This forthcoming academic year, among other things, we plan to concentrate our energies on encouraging students to cultivate a personal prayer-life that suits them. We hope to build on the already good connections with the Support Services, and look for new opportunities to reach out to those students who feel the Church has nothing relevant to offer them.

Why not visit the Chaplaincy website at: http://www.ex.ac.uk/chaplaincy/ or the CathSoc website at: http://gosh.ex.ac.uk/societies/catholic"

We may add to Canon Cummins' report the observable effect upon the congregation at Sunday masses at Sacred Heart Church of term time and vacation. Many undergraduates help in parish activities such as the choir, but plainly their participation is limited to their residence in Exeter. Permanently resident parishioners welcome students joining them as worshippers and as sharers in social life for those who choose to. Chaplaincies are specifically geared to the rhythm of academic study and research, and include contact with departments of theology.

Those of us who have benefitted from the advice and support of a University chaplaincy will not forget how great is our debt to those involved.

Fig 26   *Good Friday Walk of Witness, 2002*
[Express & Echo]

Anyone examining differences in parish attitudes since 1984 would be struck by the progress made in working with other Christians in the Exeter area. We have already reviewed various aspects of this work in previous chapters. Sacred Heart Parish plays a full part in the work of Christians Together in Central Exeter. One of the three Sacred Heart representatives on that body, Pat Murphy, has taken a turn since 2004 at being its honorary secretary. It promotes such events as the (revived) Good Friday Walk of Witness around Exeter, occasional joint services, sharing information about activities undertaken in each member church, Lenten house Groups, Songs of Praise on the Quay and Christmas Carols in High Street. Another example of joint action on an ecumenical basis has been the support for the range of services at Palace Gate Centre, originally a Baptist initiative, and the creation of St. Petroc's as a centre for homeless people. A number of new schemes under the heading of "Exeter Community Initiatives" have evolved from the Palace Gate scheme and parish interest in them has been maintained.

A list of the Christians Together in Central Exeter is as follows:

Central Parish
City Community Church
Exeter Cathedral
Mint Methodist Church
Sacred Heart Roman Catholic Church

Salvation Army
Sidwell Street Methodist Church
Society of Friends
South Street Baptist Church
Southernhay United Reformed Church

Although the numbers of adherents to other faiths than Christianity are small in Exeter compared with those in other parts of Britain, it seems likely that their numbers will increase. [19] It is important, therefore, to be well informed about, for example, the faith of Hindus, Sikhs and Moslems, and seek to share common concerns with them as citizens. [18] Those of the Moslem faith are comparatively well represented and visible in Exeter by an established mosque and through the University Centre of Arabic and Islamic Studies. (In 2004 a lecturer from the Centre accepted an invitation to explain the Moslem faith at the Cardinal Newman Centre). Less well known to local parishioners, and less in numbers, are those of the Jewish faith, whose small synagogue is close to South Street. Yet at every offering of the Mass in Sacred Heart Church (as elsewhere) the celebrant invokes God's blessing in these words: "look with favour on these offerings, and accept them as once you accepted the gifts of your servant Abel, the sacrifice of Abraham, our father in faith, and the bread and wine offered by your priest Melchisedech." This continuity of scripture is emphasised in the Apostolic Letter for the year of the Eucharist 2004-5 - "In the account of the disciples on the road to Emmaus, Christ himself intervenes to show 'beginning with Moses and all the prophets' how 'all the Scriptures' point to the mystery of this person." [36.3]

Whilst remaining unequivocally committed to their own church, Catholics do share worship with other Christians where it is appropriate to do so. Some parishioners prefer to learn to understand differences between Christian traditions and to respect them, whilst praying for eventual unity, rather than favour artificially confected liturgy which may mask genuine differences. The latter type of joint liturgy may be based on unintentional sentimentality or might lead to the error of indifferentism. "The desire to come together as brothers must not lead to a watering down or a whittling away of truth" (Pope Paul VI). "There is a need," writes Monsignor Roderick Strange of the Beda College in Rome, "to maintain a climate of trust so that whatever might appear as a loss is recognised as a gain when unity is the prize and the prize is won." (Times, Jan. 24th 2004) Mary Ann James, the Bishop's Ecumenical Officer for Devon, reminds us of "the strong lead and prominent role played by Bishop Christopher Budd in taking his turn among the traditions to serve as chairman of Christians Together in Devon… and the open Forum of Church Leaders in Devon." [12]

What internal machinery should operate in parishes like ours to ensure effective consultation between people, priests, other religious and the bishop? How will honest evaluation of the effectiveness of parish pastoral councils turn out? What alternative structures should be considered in the quest for greater consultation within the dioceses of the Catholic Church as advocated by Cardinal Cormac Murphy-O'Connor, reported in the Tablet in November 2004? These questions will have to be faced in the new century.

The success, even the existence, of any organised structure for bringing together parishioners for consultation and co-operation in parish affairs depends upon a favourable attitude of the parish priest. It also depends upon enough interest on the part of parishioners in sufficient number to ensure that genuine consultation is effected and that the error is avoided of having largely self-selected spokespersons deciding what is good for everyone else. Informal consultation among parishioners and published literature about parish organisation leads one to that unsurprising conclusion. (P.2, P.10, 18, 32)

In Sacred Heart parish our records of Parish Council meetings are incomplete, but it is clear that a proposal to form such a body had been considered in 1970. A letter to parishioners from Fr. Frank Balment (as he then was) dated June 29th 1971 announces a meeting at Palace Gate Convent on July 5th to form a Parish Council. A draft outline constitution gives the purpose of the Council as "to work with the parish priest in the furtherance of the spiritual and temporal welfare of the parish." The parish priest is given as chairman of the Council, and the membership consists of any other priests of the parish, twelve representatives of each of the major groups and associations in the parish, and twelve elected members from an annual parish meeting, half of whom retire each year. Among the submissions to the parish priest and to the parish general meeting was a detailed proposal from John Kewell, most of whose ideas were taken up in the eventual constitution, duly adopted unanimously on July 5th 1971. (P.2)

By December 1971 the Parish Council announced its decision to produce a monthly bulletin with a full account of parish activities. Committees of the Council had been formed on functional lines: Spiritual and Religious, Social and Welfare, Financial. The latter committee proposed to introduce "a system of planned giving or stewardship as it is sometimes called." The honorary secretary is listed as Mr. D.L.B. Thomas, the Hon. Treasurer as Mr. J.P. Connolly (a local bank manager) and Professor R.A.B. Leaper as the Vice-Chairman. A number of other people still very active in the parish in 2004 are listed in the membership of the committees. Two new roles in the liturgy were announced for the first time in the Parish Council bulletin in March 1972: the appointment of lay readers (a little later women readers) and a rota for bringing the offertory gifts to the celebrant during Mass. An education committee was formed in January 1973 as part of the Parish Council to join with other parishes in advancing the cause of Catholic Secondary education in the Exeter area. In view of later developments for children it is interesting to read the minutes of a lively debate at a Parish Council meeting in 1973 about the setting up of a crèche in the newly renovated Lower Room of the Presbytery. A wide range of subjects, including the installation of contraceptive vending machines in town continued to pre-occupy the Council through the following years, the elected officers continuing to rotate, as the constitution laid down.

Full details of the income and expenditure of the parish were provided by the parish priest to the financial committee and then to parishioners in the Bulletin. A planned giving campaign was introduced by Fr. Keith Collins after he succeeded Canon Frank Balment as parish priest. By 1983 we read of thanks being expressed by Fr. Collins to Robert Leaper and Jo O'Mahony for their tenures of office as vice-chairman and to Fred O'Keefe succeeding as Hon. Sec. and Michael Penny as

Treasurer (the latter to be elected as chairman of the later Parish Pastoral Council). Michael Penny as Treasurer devoted a great deal of time and energy to raising funds for repairs to the church roof, and to obtaining grants towards the work from central and local government bodies. The Unity Commission was the body formed to foster ecumenical activity and Neville Simpson and Ron Tamplin are recorded as Sacred Heart Parish representatives. Throughout the years under review the "Parish Council of the Church of the Sacred Heart Exeter" had its own headed writing paper on which many letters signed by the Parish Priest or the Hon. Sec. were addressed to a range of statutory and Christian organisations.

From March 1984 there are no notes of any meetings of a Parish Council until the formation of the Parish Pastoral Council now active from 1999. In the interim, however, there were three meetings of representatives of parish activities groups convened with the purpose of achieving greater co-operation, more publicity for the groups and more recruitment to them. This culminated in an "activities fair" on February 6th 2002 where all the main groups in the parish had stands and at which Professor Margaret Green spoke as the then chairperson of the Diocesan Pastoral Council.

The constitution of the "Exeter Sacred Heart Pastoral Council" resulted from consultation between the Parish Priest, Michael Penny (having a legal background) and one or two other parishioners with experience of similar bodies both in this parish and elsewhere. It also took account of the Plymouth Diocesan Vision Statement as promulgated by Bishop Christopher Budd. "The purpose of the Council," states its constitution, "will be to provide in a consultative capacity and in accordance with the code of Canon Law, the opportunity whereby the body of Christ's faithful meet to share the responsibility of the whole parish life and of the whole community." These lofty aims are then spelt out in some detail and the composition of the council is described as consisting of: the "Parish Team," that is the clergy and religious working in the parish as named by the parish priest, representatives of each of the organisations active in the parish, up to ten parishioners elected by a parishioners' meeting, and an allowance for a small number of co-options. Adopting common practice in voluntary bodies in civic life, there is a limitation on the length of office held by the elected membership. The constitution envisaged the appointment of an "Information Officer / Co-ordinator" (a function efficiently performed by the late John Curran). This has now been superseded by the appointment in 2003 of a parish secretary who among other duties assures the secretarial management of the Council. Updating of computerised services in the parish office has greatly improved efficiency. Within the Council's operations the membership has been divided into four groups each related to a four-fold specification in the Bishop's "Vision Statement" - the celebrating church, the caring church, the learning church, the living church.

Fig 27 *Parish art work festival, 2000*

Fig 28 *Parish summer garden party at Cardinal Newman Centre, 2004*
(Mount St. Mary's Convent in the background)

The Parish Pastoral Council has proved a useful vehicle for sharing information and fostering better co-operation, but as a focus of inspiration or decision-making it has a long way to go. This seems to be especially the case as a means of two-way communication between the parish and the rest of the diocese. The Council's own representatives on the Deanery Council have been particularly critical of this element in Diocesan consultative machinery. The four-fold categorisation of groups within the Council has also been questioned as a means of effective action, and the lack of clear and frequent publicity about the council's membership and work may account for an apparently tepid parish enthusiasm. At diocesan level the Vicar-General, Monsignor Robert Draper, has been considering possible models for involvement and effective advice between parishes and diocesan bodies and John Manix, of the Diocesan Department of Formation, has been involved in preparing a document on alternative strategies for effective parish involvement in consultation. It is to be hoped that any such documentation will draw upon the wide range of experience and writing in the community work field so as to avoid reinventing the wheel. Its application to the daily realities of parish life will demand scrutiny and debate at parish level before final guidance emerges. The debate has already started in the Catholic press and in documentation from the Conference of Bishops. It seems likely to be carried on in Sacred Heart parish over the next decade.

The Bishops' Conference of England & Wales embarked in 2004 on a project for the "U.N. Year of the Family." A leaflet was widely distributed throughout all dioceses. It contained three sets of questions about family difficulties, family blessings, societal pressures on families, and potential support and help from the church. Respondents were encouraged to share discussion in small groups, respecting confidentiality. Sacred Heart parish agreed to participate; attention was drawn to the leaflets and parishioners were encouraged to complete them and return them within three weeks. The Plymouth diocesan contact person, the Reverend Tony Irwin, undertook the compilation of the responses, some of which came to him through parish priests, some directly to him, and some after other discussion processes. This unfortunately makes it impossible to extract the responses specific to Sacred Heart parish and to compare them with other parishes. The results were reported and their significance discussed at a "Family Listening Day" at Buckfast Abbey on October 9th 2004. A report of the day, including a summary of responses, is to be reviewed by Bishop Budd and a full diocesan report is expected in 2005, followed by a national one shortly afterwards. Bishop John Hine, Chairman of the Bishops' Committee for Marriage and Family Life, had commented at the outset of the whole exercise: "So many things have changed - the place of women in society, the role of men, there is much more emphasis on leisure and yet work appears more and more demanding... If the church, the people of God, are going to minister to each other, we need to understand what the real needs of families are today." Elizabeth Davies, project officer at national level, emphasised the need for marriage preparation and help to families at local level, and those needs were substantially endorsed in another diocesan enquiry to parish priests.

In the event the outcome of the "Listening 2004" family survey in Plymouth Diocese was numerically disappointing. 15,450 brochures were distributed to the 129 churches in the Diocese, but there was a response rate of only 3%. The results must therefore be treated prudently, but the material amassed will form useful references for parish priests and parish pastoral councils in their work in support of families. Of those who responded, one clear result from the survey was that there should be more publicity at parish level about the services available to those with family problems, and that confidentiality must be most carefully protected. Elizabeth Davies commented after the Day at Buckfast that "A need for stronger, more cohesive parish communities, increased opportunities for adult education and a broader understanding of marriage preparation" were among its conclusions. A brief account of the "Listening 2004" family survey by Robert Leaper, as a participant, appeared in the monthly "Catholic South West" in December 2004.

In June 1994 there was published the report of a working party chaired by Bishop Christopher Budd on behalf of the Catholic Bishop's Conference whose preface reads: "During the past decade the increased public awareness of Child Abuse in its many forms and enduring consequences, has led government departments to combine their resources to sharpen the principles and policy by which this evil could be resisted…The Catholic Community in England and Wales has become increasingly aware of incidents when persons who hold positions of responsibility within the Church, including priests, have abused young people, physically, sexually, emotionally and by neglect." [P.10] The report examined frankly and thoroughly all aspects of the wrong-doing and of any proposed action to combat it. The report carried considerable weight from its authority and provenance, though it had been preceded by a modest document emanating from the Advisory Committee for child care of the (now replaced) Plymouth Diocesan Committee for Social Care, chaired by Dame Catherine Hall DBE. The committee had set out four forms of child abuse within the general context of "The Church and Child Care" (1994), and it unambiguously recommended resort to the statutory child protection services - or the police in emergency, while recognising the use of confidential reference within the church's own structure. This has been during a period of widespread media publicity on child abuse in Church in the United States and in Ireland as well as in Britain, strong criticism being expressed over alleged attempts to deal with the incidents exclusively within Church institutions. [23.3]

The Bishop's Conference then established an independent review committee on child protection under the chairmanship of Lord Nolan, whose final report appeared in 2001. Written evidence to the Nolan committee was given from individuals in Sacred Heart Parish. The Nolan review made 83 recommendations, covering thoroughly the whole question of child protection and child abuse in the Church, whilst reminding us of the sad fact that "Most abuse takes place in the family or in other contexts outside the church." In January 2003 there was established the "Catholic Office for the Protection of Children and Vulnerable Adults." It advises the Bishops' Conference and those directly working with the population identified in its title, and it follows the Nolan recommendations, including that of avoiding the impression of restricting to internal investigation or solution any cases of alleged abuse.

The Plymouth Diocesan Yearbook reports the appointment of a Diocesan Child Protection Commission with a Diocesan Child Protection Officer (Chris Jarvis). [P.4] In Sacred Heart parish there is a voluntary child protection worker, Chris Miller. [P.2] These provisions will be kept under review as child protection work in the country generally proceeds through the responses of social services and police to adult abuse of children.

The other half of the work of the Catholic Office mentioned above concerns the protection of "vulnerable adults" and it is much less well developed. The Office initiated consultations on the well-being of people in later life in 2004 with a conference on "Ageing Disgracefully" at which Sacred Heart parish was represented.

Some parishioners are also actively involved in a series of seminars throughout Devon run by the Christian Group on Ageing which brings together for consultation and review Christians of all denominations working with and for people in later life - whether in their own home, in residences or in hospital and nursing homes. The conclusions from these seminars will be recorded in a publication due to appear in 2005. Clergy and laypersons who regularly visit parishioners unable to attend Mass in church will need to consider this publication and its potential help in further developing work with an increasing percentage of local parishioners over the next decade. It will be important to work out programmes to involve children and young parishioners in the life of the parish without implying a neglect of those in later life. How to ensure that each involves the other will continue to demand attention.

Fig 29   *Youth SVP celebrate, 2004*

"We grow from our past" comments Eamon Duffy, [23.3] "and we only flourish when we are in touch with that past...Faithfulness to that tradition is not a matter of uncritical obedience to authority; it is a shared labour of learning, in which we work together to draw new and surprising growth from the old soil."

Parishioners of Sacred Heart have a great deal to be thankful for - and many have said so in conversation. There are some temporary disappointments and some continuing challenges: in the recent decline in mass attendance, in the drift away of some from the Faith, in the lukewarm response to the call to engage in evangelisation. There will doubtless be renewed discussion of the new English translation of the liturgy. The Catholic Truth Society leaflet "Introducing the Revised General Instruction of the Roman Missal" (2005) prepares us for the latest changes. A revised edition of full "General Instruction" was published in April 2005. An accompanying text, "Celebrating the Mass," has been issued by the Bishops of England and Wales. Both documents demand study and implementation at parish level. (Published by Catholic Truth Society)

Fig 30 *Ordination to the Priesthood of Martin Rossman, 6ᵗʰ May 2005
by Bishop Christopher Budd.*
[James Millmore]

In recounting some of the story of the Catholic parish of Sacred heart, Exeter we have touched on a varied, and at times turbulent, history of Christians associating primarily for worship of and thanksgiving to God. We have focused on a defined geographic and administrative unit with a particular form of human association but of divine inspiration and sustenance. The evidence shows that the parish has been, and still is, significant to the large majority of those who worship together, so that their association spills over into a range of connected activities. Friendships have been found, families have worked together through difficulties and celebrated happily, children have been baptised into the Faith and generations have made their First Communions and been confirmed here, others have been mourned and buried from here. Some parishioners still alive have been through almost all those experiences! The parish and its church may not have been the only focus in parishioners' lives, but it has been a significant one for very many - even today when greater mobility and social change put a premium on novelty. Even if we remain chary (as in the Author's Preface) of loosely using the word "community," Sacred Heart Parish still has some important elements of that concept in the lives of its members. Change challenges parishioners, but a sense of parish continuity gives confidence in facing that change.

Fig 31 *The Christmas Crib*

APPENDIX A

<u>CHURCH SERVICES 2005</u>

Sunday Mass Times	Saturday 5:30 p.m.
	Sunday 9:30 a.m.
	11:00 a.m.
Weekday Mass	10:00 a.m.
Wednesday Mass at Royal Devon and Exeter Hospital	4:00 p.m.

Confession (Saturdays)	After 10:00 a.m. Mass and 3:00 - 4:00 p.m.
Rosary	After Mass each Weekday
Morning Prayer	9:45 a.m. each Weekday

There are extra services in Holy Week, Eastertide, and Christmastide for which see special notices in the church porch.

APPENDIX B

PRIMARY REFERENCE SOURCES

(In the references marked in the text, primary sources are marked with an initial "P"; secondary sources are marked with numbers only.)

1. Notes on parish services and events compiled by Mr. Laurence McWilliam 1934 - 1981.

2. Documentation on the Parish Council 1972 - 83, Parish Pastoral Council 200 - 04.

3. Chapel Book of St. Nicholas Chapel, the Mint 1775 - 1836.

4. Plymouth Diocesan Yearbook 1954 et seq.

5. Exeter Deanery Clergy Conference Book 1918 - 1950.

6. Sacred Heart Choir Journal 1913 - 1919.

7. Record Book of the meetings of Managers (later Governors) of St. Nicholas R.C. School 1956 - 1998.
    All the above documents have been consulted in Sacred Heart Church parish archives, by courtesy of Monsignor Harry Doyle.

8. Bendall, R et al. The Story of Catholic Exeter. Exeter Catholic Study Group. (1964).

9. Annals of the Convent of Presentation of Mary, Exeter.

10. Archives of the Diocese of Plymouth (now at Dartmouth, Canon Smith, Diocesan Archivist).

11. Gabb, Arthur. A History of Baptist Beginnings. South Street Baptist Church. (1956).

12. Issues of Trewman's Exeter Flying Post 1880 - 1914 (in Library of the Devon and Exeter Institution). Also Exeter Flying Post 2000 - 2004.

13. Issues of Western Times 1831 - 1881. (same source)

14. Issues of Devon and Exeter Gazette 1887 - 1914. (same source)

15. Issues of Express and Echo 1945 et seq. (by courtesy of West Country Research Centre, Exeter). Also Express and Echo issues for 1923.

16. Issues of Exeter Catholic Magazine 1953 and 1956.

17. Issues of South Western Catholic History. 1983 et seq. Downside Abbey.

18. Milsom, Sr. Edward Mary, and Sandiford, Carol. Mount Saint Mary School. (1996)

19. Sundry MSS. by Reverend Dr. George Oliver (in the University of Exeter Catholic Chaplaincy Library, by courtesy of Canon Paul Cummins).

20. Plymouth Diocesan Record. 1933 - 39. Plymouth Diocesan Archives.

21. The Documents of Vatican II. Ed. Walter M. Abbott. Geoffrey Chapman. (1966).

22. Oral evidence from Monsignor Harry Doyle, Canon Francis Balment, Rev. Father Keith Collins, Canon Bernard Jaffa.

REFERENCES

1. Allan, John. St. Nicholas Priory, Exeter. Exeter City Council. 1999.

2. Andrews, John et al. Exeter Coinage. University of Exeter. 1980.

3. Anglo-Saxon Chronicle. (Ed. and Trans.) James Ingram. J.M. Dent. 1912.
    (Ed. and Trans.) Dorothy Whitelock et al. London. 1961.

4. Avis, Paul. The Anglican Understanding of the Church. SPCK. 2000.

5. Barber, Chips. The Lost City of Exeter. Obelisk. 1982.

6. Barclay, Peter M. Social Workers: their role and tasks. Bedford Square Press.
    1989.

7. Barlow, Frank. Leofric of Exeter. Exeter University Press. 1972.

8. Barry, Michael. By pen and pulpit. Satum Books, Cork. 1990.

9. Basherville, G. English monks and the suppression of the monasteries. London.
    1937.

10. Bidwell, Paul T. Roman Exeter. Exeter University Press. 1980.

11. Black, Jeremy. Georgian Devon. Mint Press. 2003.

12. Budd, Christopher, Bishop. Vision in Action. Diocese of Plymouth. 2003.

13. Catholic Agency for Social Concern. Community Care: the Challenge for the
    Catholic Church. CASC. 2000.

14. Catholic Bishops Conference of England & Wales, Cherishing Life. Colloquium.
    2004.

15. Charity Commission. 1) The Hallmarks of an effective charity (CC 60). 2001.
    2) Membership Charities (RS7). 2001.

16. Clifton-Taylor, Alec. The Cathedrals of England. Thomas & Hudson. 1967.

17. Coleman, B. I. "Exeter in the census of religious worship, 1851" in Devon
    Historian, 23. 1981.

18. Coleman, Simon & Collins, Peter. Religion, Identity and Change. Ashgate.
    2004.

19. Davie, Grace. Religion in Britain since 1945. Blackwell. 1994.

20. Davies, Bleddyn et al. Community Care in England and France. Ashgate. 1998.

21. Davies, Hilery. Catholics in Crediton. St. Boniface Church, Crediton. 1999.

22. Duby, Georges. France in the Middle Ages. Blackwell. 1999.

23. Duffy, Eamon. 1) The Voices of Morebath. Yale University Press. 2001.
                 2) The Stripping of the Altars. Yale University Press. 1992.
                 3) Faith of our fathers. Continuum. 2004.

24. Erskine, Audrey et al. Exeter Cathedral, a short history and description. Exeter Cathedral. 1988.

25. Farwell, Eddie. Focus on Devon. Devon County Council. 2004.

26. Fortescue, Adrian. The Ceremonies of the Roman Rite Described. Burns & Oates. 1918.

27. Fox, Aileen. 1) Exeter in Roman Times. Exeter University. 1971.
              2) Roman Exeter. Manchester University Press. 1952.

28. Furet, Francois. Revolutionary France 1770-1880. Blackwell. 1999.

29. Graham, Bishop Charles. History of Plymouth Diocese. (MS.) 1912.

30. Gray, Todd. 1) The Victorian Under-class of Exeter. Mint Press. 2001.
             2) Victorian Stories of Exeter. Mint Press. 2001.
             3) Exeter Unveiled. Mint Press. 2003.
             4) Exeter Engraved. Mint Press. 2001.
             5) Lost Exeter - Five centuries of change. Mint Press. 2002.
             6) Exeter in the 1940s. Mint Press. 2004.

31. Holden, Marcus. Saints of the English Calendar. Family Publications. 2004.

32. Hornsby-Smith (Ed.) Catholics in England 1950-2000. Cassell. 1999.

33. Hoskins, W.G. 1) Two thousand years in Exeter. 1960.
               2) Devon. David & Charles. 1972.
               3) Two thousand years in Exeter. New edition edited by Hazel Harvey. Phillimore. 2004.

34. Jacobsen, Walter. Around the Churches of Devon. Obelisk. 1998.

35. John XXIII, Pope. Mater et Magistra. Catholic Truth Society. 1961.

36. John Paul II, Pope. 1) Catechism of the Catholic Church. Geoffrey Chapman. 1994.
                  2) Redemptionis Sacramentum. CTS. 2004.
                  3) Mane Nobiscum Domine. CTS. 2004.
                    (Abide with us, Lord)

37. Jones, Keith. Exeter Cathedral - a guide for visitors. Scala Publishers. 2004.

38. Kennedy, Paul. The Catholic Church in England & Wales 1500 - 2000. PBK. 2001.

39. Knowles, David & Obolensky, Dimitri. The Middle Ages. Darton, Longman & Todd. 1979.

40. Ladurie, Emmanuel Le Roy. The Royal French State. 1460 - 1610. Blackwell. 1944.

41. Leaper, R.A.B. 1) Community Work. National Council of Social Service. 1971
    2) National Pastoral Congress in Retrospect in <u>The Tablet</u>. 28 June, 1980.
    3) & MacWilliam, Laurence. Change & Continuity - an Exeter Centenary, Exeter 1984.
    4) The Beveridge Report in its contemporary setting. International Social Security Review. 1992.

42. Little, Bryan. Exeter. Batsford. 1953.

43. MacGrath, K. M. Catholicism in Devon and Cornwall, 1767 in Buckfast Chronicle. Vol. 30. No. 3. 1960.

44. Miller, Edward. A History of the College of St. John the Evangelist in Cambridge. Cambridge University Press. 1961.

45. Minchinton, Walter. Life of the city. Devon Books. 1987.

46. Mitchell, Duncan (Ed.) A new dictionary of Sociology. Routledge, Kegan Paul. 1979.

47. Monro, Margaret T. St. Margaret Clitherow. Family Publications. 2004.

48. Murphy-O'Connor, Cormac. At the Heart of the World. Darton, Longman & Todd. 2004.

49. Newton, Robert. Victorian Exeter. Leicester University Press. 1968.

50. Oliver, George. 1) Ed. Dom John Stephen. The Ancient Religious Houses of Devon. Buckfast Abbey. 1935.
    2) Ecclesistical Antiquities in Devon (3 vols.) Featherstone. 1840.
    3) History of the city of Exeter. 1861.

51. Orme, Nicholas. 1) Exeter Cathedral as it was. 1050-1550. Devon Books. 1986. (O.P.)
    2) (Ed.) Unity & Variety - a History of the Church in Devon and Cornwall. Exeter University Press. 1991.

52. Parry, H. Lloyd et al. St. Nicholas Priory, Exeter. W. J. Southward. 1917.

53. Paul VI, Pope. Gaudium et Spes. Catholic Truth Society. 1986.

54. Percy, Martin. The Changing Identity of the English Parish Church in Religion, Identity and Change (Ed.). Coleman & Collins. Ashgate. 2004.

55. Plymouth Diocesan Trust. Annual Report and Accounts. 2003.

56. Pontifical Council. The Church and the Elderly. Vatican City Press. 1999.

57. Raymond, Mary Ruth. Street - names of Exeter. Obelisk Publications. 2000.

58. Reed, Alcuin OSB. The organic development of the liturgy. St. Michael's Abbey Press. 2004.

59. Reynolds, E.G. Saint John Fisher. 1955.

60. Rigby, Cormac. The Lord be with you. Family Publications. 2003.

61. Roots, Ivor. Cromwellian & Restoration Devon. Mint Press. 2003.

62. Rose-Troup, Frances. 1) Exeter Vignettes. Manchester University Press. 1942.
    2) Lost Chapels of Exeter. Manchester University Press. 1923.

63. St. Leger-Gordon, D. Portrait of Devon. Robert Hale. 1963.

64. Scarisbrook, J.T. Henry VIII. Oxford University Press. 1976.

65. Schama, Simon. A History of Britain. Vol. 1. B.B.C. Worldwide. 2000.

66. Scherer, Jacqueline. Contemporary Community. Tavistock. 1972.

67. Sladden, J.C. Boniface of Devon. Paternoster Press. 1980.

68. Slader, J.M. Churches of Devon. 1965.

69. Snell, Lawrence S. The Suppression of the Religious Foundations of Devon and Cornwall. Wordens. 1967.

70. Spencer, Nick. Parochial Vision. Paternoster. 2004.

71. Stephan, Dom John. Church of St. Boniface, Crediton. 1969.

72. Stoyle, Mark. Circled with Stone. Exeter University Press. 2004.

73. Susser, B. The Jews of South-West England. Exeter. 1841.

74. Sykes, Stephen. Power in the Church of England in <u>Concilium</u>. T. & T. Clark. 1988.

75. Thomas, David N. The Making of Community Work. Allen & Urwin. 1983.

76. Thomas, Peter. 1) Exeter Yesterday and Today. Sutton Publishing. 2000.
    2) Exeter The Golden Years. Halsgrove. 2003.

77. Thompson, Arthur Huxley. The story of Exeter Cathedral. Raphael Tuck. 1933.

78. Venn, Gilbert. St. Leonard's. Exeter Civic Society. 1982.

79. Walsh, James. Forty Martyrs of England & Wales. Catholic Truth Society. 1997.

80. Watkin, E. I. Roman Catholicism in England. O.U.P. 1957.

81. Willmott, Peter. Community Initiatives. Policy Studies Institute. 1989.

82. Yoder, J.A. & Leaper, R.A.B. Support Networks in a Caring Community. Nijhoff. 1985.

83. Youings, Joyce. 1) St. Nicholas Priory. Exeter City Council. 1960.
    2) Tuckers Hall Exeter University. 1968.

APPENDIX C

<u>INVENTORY OF PHOTOGRAPHS</u>

Front Cover: Sacred Heart Church exterior in Exeter City Centre

1. High Altar, sanctuary, reredos and rood screen
2. St. Edward the Confessor, St. Walburga
3. The Baptistery
4. The Lady Altar
5. Statue of St. Thomas More
6. St. Boniface Altar and Window
7. Sacred Heart Church, The Presbytery, Cathedral Tower, Baptist Church
8. The Banner of the Five Wounds - 1549 Prayer Book Rising
9. Dr. George Oliver
10. Interior of St. Nicholas Chapel, The Mint - end of 19th Century
11. Mint Chapel Memorial Plaque
12. The church tower with wooden cap
13. Blessed Sacrament procession, Palace Gate - early 1920s (?)
14. Parish procession at the Guildhall with Fr. Balment, 1938
15. Polish airmen present their flag to the city, 1942
16. Procession up South Street - post-war ruins, 1945
17.. Hierarchy Centenary 1850 - 1950, Pontifical High Mass, Sacred Heart Church
18. Pontifical High Mass, 1950. Bishop Grimshaw
19. Commemoration of the anniversary of the Western Rising, 1949
20 The church choir in 1972 with Harold Stringer
21. Palace Gate Convent and School
22. The chapel at Palace Gate Convent School
23. St. Thomas of Canterbury Church, Dunsford Road
24. A cheque towards the cost of roof repairs - Fr. Bernard Jaffa, 1988
25. Altar servers with Monsignor Harry Doyle, 2000
26. Good Friday Walk of Witness, 2002
27. Parish art work festival, 2000
28. Parish summer garden party at Cardinal Newman Centre, 2004
29. Youth SVP celebrate, 2004
30. Ordination to the Priesthood of Martin Rossman, May 6th, 2005 by Bishop Christopher Budd.
31. The Christmas Crib

APPENDIX D

<u>LIST OF PARISH PRIESTS</u>

In the Chapel Book, whose contents were compiled by Dr. George Oliver, there appear the following notes of the parish priests and their predecessors at the Mint Chapel. These were from "documents in the hands of the Jesuit Fathers", writes Dr. Oliver.

<u>Rev. John Reeve</u> We know that the Rev. John Reeve had been instituted on 15 July 1558 by Dr. Turberville, the last Catholic Bishop of Exeter to the vicarage of Alternun in Cornwall, but was deprived of his benefice in the early part of Elizabeth's reign. He was subsequently apprehended & brought before Bishop Wootton, a bitter enemy of Catholics in his palace here on 24 March 1581: the said bishop certified to the Queen's Bench on the 19th of the ensuing month that the fugitive Priest had refused *peremptoris et obstinate tunc et ibidem*, "to take the oath of Supremacy". He was tried & condemned on 31 March 1582 & two days later was executed at Chelmsford.

<u>Rev. Thomas Laithwite</u> After six months captivity 1604 in our county jail, under Exeter Castle was banished. He died 10 June 1655.

<u>Rev. John Sweet</u> was apprehended in this city on 14 Nov. 1621 & after suffering close imprisonment till 11 Dec. was conducted to London by order of the Privy Council. He died 26 Feb. 1632.

<u>Rev. Thos Bullakee</u> was a prisoner here during the winter of 1630 & finally received the crown of martyrdom at London on 12 Oct. 1642.

<u>Fr. Richard Norris S.J.</u> During the short reign of James II, a chapel nicknamed by Calamy "a mass house" was opened, but it was so completely demolished at the Revolutionary explosion that its local situation has not been discovered. It was served by <u>Fr. Richard Norris S.J.</u> who narrowly escaped with his life. He survived till 21 June 1717. After this nothing can be gleamed but that a priest occasionally visited the Catholics of this city.

<u>Visiting Priests</u> An old man John Flood, who was born in Exeter 16 Feb. 1724 & died at the age of 91, said that the service was performed in an upper room of W. Flashman's house, commonly called King John's entry in South Street, that he had known the <u>Rev. J. Beaumont</u> OSF, the <u>Rev. E. Hussey</u> OSB who died 25 Sept. 1786 and the secular clergyman <u>Rev. Edward Williams</u> who died at Beasiscombe (sic) 30 Jan. 1776, the <u>Revs Parry & Rigby</u>, & the <u>Rev Wm Sutton</u> who closed his life at Axminster at a very advanced age on 23 Jan. 1800.

Fr. William Gillibrand S.J. The Jesuits offer to Bishop Walmsley to provide a resident pastor for the remnant of Catholicity in Exeter. Their first missionary was Fr. William Gillibrand S.J. who seems to have arrived late in 1792 or early 1793 & to have boarded with a Catholic of the name of Truscott in Exe Island near the present Gas Works. The Rev. Father left Exeter after about 5 years residence to take possession of the family estate at Chorley & there died 22 March 1779.

Fr. Anthony Carroll S.J. Succeeded in 1779 & served the Chapel for two years. He died from accident in London 5 Sept. 1771 (probably 1781- G.O.)

Fr. Joseph Barrow S.J. was sent late in 1771 from Tasmore to replace Fr. Carroll. After a twelve month he was transferred to Arlington, but on July 1, 1786 he reached St. Helens' where he laboured till he died 1813.

Fr. John Edisford S.J. was translated from Salisbury on Fr. Barrow's retirement & for 17 years carefully cultivated his vineyard. He died of jail fever in attending the prisoners in the old county jail on Sat. 20, Nov. 1789 & according to the parochial register of S. Olave was buried in the Church 24 Nov.

Fr. William Poole S.J. was the next resident priest for the same period as his predecessor. He was then removed to Bulford near Leigh Co. Lancaster & there ended his days 27 Feb 1828.

Fr. Thomas Lewis S.J. was then called from Chideock in Jan. 1807 & continued until Oct. that year when he returned to his former mission & there died 5 Sept 1809.

Rev. George Oliver succeeded Fr. Lewis in Oct. 1807. HH Pope Gregory XVI was pleased to confer upon him the degree of DD on 15 Sept. 1844. He died & is buried in the Catholic Chapel Exeter.

Fr. James Eccles S.J. succeeded on 6 Oct. 1851 & was removed Oct. 1861.

Fr. McCann S.J. succeeded & was removed Sept. 1863.

Fr. Wm. Johnson S.J. succeeded on Sept. 9, 1863 & was removed Dec. 1871. He was succeeded by two secular priests W. Hobson and W. Richie.

(end of extract from George Oliver's notes from the Jesuit Fathers)

From 1871 we know from various other documents (see the reference section) that the following is the list of parish priests, down to 2005.

1871 - 1911	**Rt. Reverend Provost W. Hobson**
1911 - 1914	**Canon C. Gandy**
1914 - 1918	**Canon J. Shepherd**
1918 - 1947	**Fr. T. Barney**
1947 - 1967	**Rt. Reverend Provost P. Tobin**
1967 - 1981	**Canon F. Balment**
1981 - 1986	**Fr. K. Collins**
1986 - 1990	**Canon B. Jaffa**
1990 -	**Reverend Monsignor H. Doyle**

APPENDIX E

PARISH APPOINTMENTS 2005

PARISH TEAM

Parish Priest: Monsignor Harry Doyle
Assistant Priests: Fr. Michael Wheaton
                          Fr. David Williams (Retired)
Deacon: Rev. Delian Bower
Parish Sister: Sr. Anna Maria Cullen

READERS

S. Baker	Fred O'Keefe
S. Bemrose	Cecilia O'Keefe
S. Berggren	M. Olivant
J. Burbridge	M. Overy
V. Espig	D. Presland
B. Grant-Watson	J. Rees
J. Hennessy	N. Simpson
S. Lasok	M. Smyth
R. Leaper	H. Swinburne
M. Leech	R. Tamplin
C. MacDonald	R. Yendall
P. Oldfield	

EXTRAORDINARY MINISTERS OF HOLY COMMUNION

Sr. Anna Maria	P. Lomax
G. Bemrose	F. O'Keefe
C. Browning	M. Olivant
L. Degnan	Martin Overy
J. Doyle	Monica Overy
B. Grant-Watson	J. Prywata
S. Hills	J. Rees
C. Huppler	K. Russell
P. Kelly	N. Simpson
J. Lawes	H. Simoneau
R. Leaper	M. Smyth
C. Lee	H. Swinburne
M. Leech	R. Williams
	R. Yendall

ALTAR SERVERS

Master of Ceremonies: Nigel Power

Timothy Bemrose
Kirsten Berggren
Christopher Bick
Sophie Browning
Ben Jones
John Lawes
Rory McKenna
Andrew Munroe
Robin Phillips
Joe Prywata
Aidan Smallwood
Gabriella Smallwood
David Smith

PASTORAL COUNCIL

The Parish Team

Ray Stokes - Acting Chair
Susan Berggren - Secretary

Cecilia Browning
Jackie Burridge
Lily Degnan
Jean Doyle
Susan Hills
Sheila Jones
Robert Leaper
Margaret McCauley
Pat Murphy
Michael Olivant
Martin Overy
Maureen Ponting
Kitty Riley
Vincent Willson

APPENDIX F

PARISH ORGANISATIONS 2005

ORGANISATIONS	Blessed Sacrament	Holy Cross	Sacred Heart
Baptism	√	√	√
CAFOD	√	√	√
Catholic Youth Club	√		√
Child Protection	√	√	√
Children's Music Group	√		√
Children's Liturgy	√	√	√
Choir / Music		√	√
Church Cleaners	√	√	√
Coffee Rota / Hospitality	√	√	√
Confirmation	√	√	√
CWL	√	√	√
Diocesan Pastoral Council	√	√	√
Ecumenical Group	√	√	√
Eucharistic Ministers	√	√	√
Exeter Deanery Forum	√	√	√
Finance and Counters	√	√	√
First Communion	√	√	√
Flower Arranging	√	√	√
Health and Safety	√	√	√
Junior SVP	√		√
KSC	√		√
LIFE	√		√
Marriage Care South West	√		√
Marriage Preparation	√	√	√
Mothers, Babies & Toddlers	√		√
Liturgy	√	√	√
Newman House Bookings			√
Palace Gate Project			√
Prayer Group	√	√	
RCIA	√		√
Readers	√	√	√
Repository			√
Sacristan	√	√	√
Servers	√	√	√
Social Group	√	√	√
Support and Liaison Group		√	
SVP	√	√	√
Welcomers	√	√	√

APPENDIX G

EXETER CATHOLIC PARISH BOUNDARIES

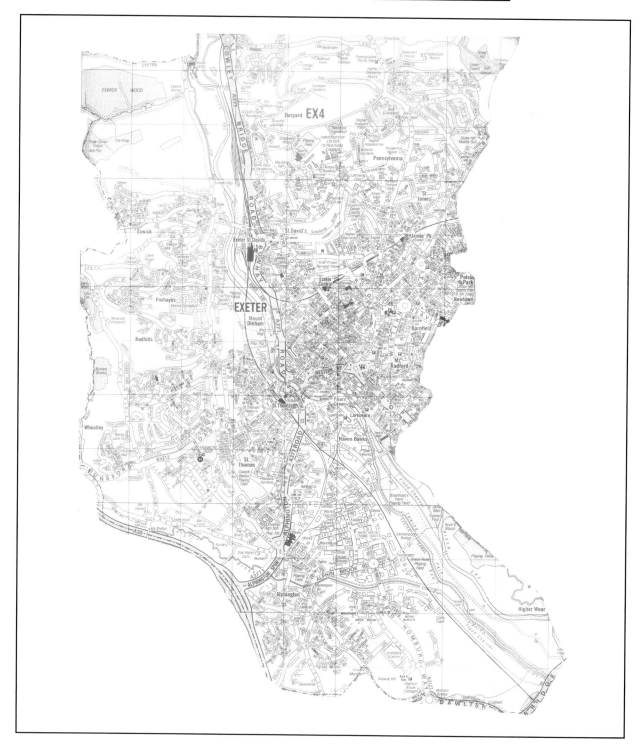

Parish of the Sacred Heart, Exeter

Parish of the Blessed Sacrament, Heavitree

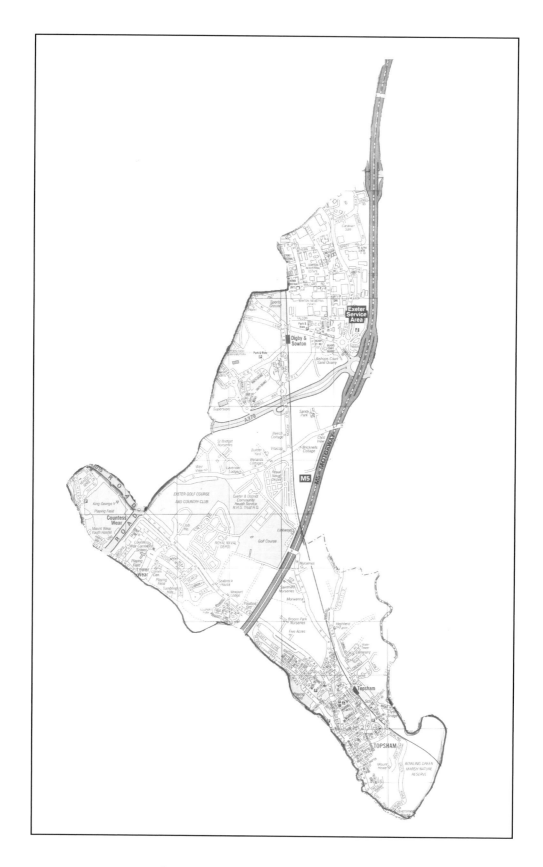

Parish of the Holy Cross, Topsham

APPENDIX H

<u>EXETER STATISTICS 2004</u>

City Population	112,000
Average Life Expectancy	
Female	80 years
Male	76 years
Population under 30 years	40%
Population over 65 years	16%
Estimated Roman Catholic Population	3550

Sources: Exeter City Council
            Plymouth Diocesan Yearbook, 2005

APPENDIX I

GENERAL INDEX

The names of present parishioners in 2005 are not included in the index. The list of parishioners with specified roles in parish activities is given in chapter 10 and the appendices; it relates to the year 2005.

Lollards, 27
Loyola, Ignatius, Saint, 26
Liddel, F., 99
Liturgy (and music), 60-2, 112
Lullus, Saint, 12
Luther, Martin, 27

MacWilliam, Laurence ("Mr. Mac"), 67, 72-3, 76, 81, 87, 89, 91, 96, 106
Manning, Henry, Cardinal, 66
Manpower Services Commission, 7, 89
Mary, Queen, 31-2
Mary Alfred, Sister, 95
Mayne, Cuthbert, Saint, 7, 32, 37
Methodist Church, 43, 60
Middleton, Miss., 6, 8, 56
Mint - passage, 16
     - chapel, 38, 42, 50, 57
     - school, 90-1
     - No.'21', 41, 52
Minster, 4
Molland, 33
Monasteries, 22-3
Moore, Harold, 81
More, Thomas, Saint, 9, 26-7
Morebath, 31
Mount St. Mary's School, 100-2, 119
Murphy O'Connor, C., Cardinal, 116
Muslim Faith, 116

Neighbourhood, 1, 65, 71, 84, 91
Newman Association, 78, 82
Newman J.H Cardinal, 49
Nicholas St., School, 51, 68, 86, 90 - 98
Nicholas Priory (St.), 10, 22-3, 27
Nolan, Lord, 121

Olaves Church, St., 22
Oliver, George Dr., 10, 18, 27, 33, 38-41, 43-4, 47-8, 51-2, 57, 83
Organ (church), 9-10
Orme, Nicholas, Professor, 4, 13, 28
O'Shaughenessy, Bernard, 84

Palace Gate (convent), 68, 70, 73, 92, 94, 98-102, 111
Parish Pastoral Council, 3, 105, 109, 113-4, 116-9
Pastoral Congress, 2, 87
Paul VI, Pope, 32, 83

APPENDIX J

GLOSSARY

    This short glossary covers a selection of commonly - used items in this book. It does not attempt authoritative definitions. The terms are described as would be commonly understood by Sacred Heart parishioners. The glossary is offered in response to requests for an explanation of unfamiliar terms by some readers of early drafts of the text.

Ambulatory: the space at the east end of the church around the chancel.

Baldacchino: a canopy supported on columns over the altar.

Boss: a covering to the intersection of ribs in a roof.

Chancel: the area at the east end of a church, often referred to in Sacred Heart church as the "the sanctuary" or "the altar".

Choir loft: the structure above the west end of the nave or above the transept, reached by stairs and used by the choir and organist.

Ciborium: the vessel used to contain the blessed sacrament hosts. (in some Anglican churches used to refer to a baldacchino-q.v)

Clerestory: windows high up in the nave.

Cruciform: (a church) built in the shape of a cross.

Gothic or Neo-Gothic: an architectural style dominant in Victorian churches, reviving a 16th century style.

Lancet: a single light window under a pointed arch.

Missal: a book containing the prayers used in the celebration of the Mass.

Minster: a grouping of practicing Christians associated with a regional church building, especially in Anglo-Saxon times.

Monstrance: a portable vessel, often richly decorated, used for displaying the Blessed Sacrament for veneration.

Mullion: the stone division between the panes of a window.

Narthex: the enclosed area at the entrance to a church.

Nave: the central part of the church building, from West to East.

Perpendicular: an architectural style dominant in churches from about 1350-1550.

Piers: stone columns dividing the nave and supporting the roof.

Pietà: a statue representing the Virgin Mary holding the body of the crucified Christ.

Piscina: a recessed basin and drain going direct to the earth, formerly for washing vessels used in eucharistic celebrations.

Presbytery: the priest's residence. (In the Cathedral the term refers to the four bays immediately in front of the high altar).

Purbeck marble: stone (not marble) from Purbeck in Dorset.

Repository: a small shop within the church dealing in books, candles, rosaries and other religious artefacts.

Reredos: a decorated screen behind and above the altar, carved in stone or other substance.

Rood: a representation in stone, wood or iron of the Crucifixion of Christ erected in front of the chancel. Before the Reformation rood screens were often substantial erections with access to and space for a choir or musicians.

Sanctuary: the area around the altar where mass is celebrated.

Sedilia: three seats side by side in either stone or wood where ministers sit at the relevant parts of the service.

Spandrel: the spaces between arches.

Spire: the apex of a tower in stone or wood tapering to a point.

Stations of the Cross: pictorial or carved representations of the fourteen stages on Christ's journey to Calvary.

Tester: an old name for a sounding board over a pulpit.

Transept: the area of the church crossing the top of the nave.

Tabernacle: has several references in various forms of Christian and Jewish worship; here refers to the small curtained cupboard used for reserving the Blessed Sacrament.

Postscript, April 2005

———— . ————

Pope John Paul II died on Saturday, April 2nd, 2005 after a long illness. Prayers had been offered for him around the world and his death was universally mourned. "He was", wrote the author of the Times obituary, "without doubt one of the most striking, interesting and influential figures of our times". The prayers composed for the Pope's death by the Catholic Bishops' Conference contain a passage asking that "Your servant John Paul, our Pope, whom you made vicar of Peter and shepherd of your church, may rejoice forever in the vision of your glory, for he was a faithful steward here on earth of the mysteries of your forgiveness and grace".

At Sacred Heart Church on that Saturday morning there were twice the number of those usually at week-day morning Mass. During all that morning, people came in off South Street asking if they could "pray for the Pope". After his death was announced, prayers for the repose of his soul were said at all the week-end Masses and then at two special memorial Masses at Exeter's two Catholic parish churches. He was well remembered too at many other churches in the city.

By order of the Acting Dean, the flag was flown at half-mast from the tower of Exeter Cathedral.

The Sacred Heart congregation prayed next for the inspiration of the Holy Spirit in the choice of the new Pope.

- On April 19th, 2005 Cardinal Joseph Ratzinger emerged from the conclave of cardinals at Vatican City as Pope Benedict XVI. -